NO ORDINARY JOE
THE LIFE AND CAREER OF JOE BIDEN

DAVID HAGAN

OPPIAN

Published by Oppian Press
Helsinki, Finland

© David Hagan 2020
All rights reserved

Cover photo by Gage Skidmore

ISBN 978-951-877-142-8

CONTENTS

'A POLITICAL MIRACLE UNLIKE ANYTHING IN MODERN PRESIDENTIAL POLITICS . . .'

It was not supposed to end like this, but there it was—a distinguished 50-year career in politics killed on a cold February night in Nashua, New Hampshire. There in the Radisson Hotel, a small crowd had gathered for what was supposed to be a watch party and a celebration, but the man they'd come to see, the man they hoped would be the next President of the United States of America, had already slunk away from the state, leaving behind an empty stage so he didn't have to face the scale of his defeat. Local reporters were scathing about his early retreat. 'He's shooting himself in the foot', one commented, 'at a time when he's already shot himself in the other foot.'

The vote that had taken place that day was the second of the 2020 primaries, the process through which the Democratic Party would select its nominee to take on Donald Trump in the November Presidential election[1]. Prior to the process starting, expert opinion had it that Joe Biden, by far the most experienced and prominent of the candidates, would win the race against a large, diverse, and mostly barely-known field.

But here, in just the second state to vote, was the supposed front-runner limping home in fifth place; beaten not just by established contenders like high-profile progressives, Bernie Sanders and Elizabeth Warren, but even by such relative political light-weights as Amy Klobuchar and Pete Buttigieg. The latter came in a very close second to the victorious Sanders, despite having never held political office higher than mayor of the tiny town of Bend, Indiana. Yet here he was, smashing the veteran former vice president of the USA, the man who had spent eight years as Barack Obama's second-in-command. Buttigieg got 24% of the vote, and Biden just 8%.

Around the nation, hacks began sharpening their pens and political obituaries were being drafted. The Washington Times called it 'The Biden Bellyflop', and for Business Insider, it was 'a huge loss, a blistering loss . . . just a week after a disastrous Iowa caucus'. The New York Times described it as 'a devastating outcome . . . [which] plunged his campaign into further peril.' 'There's blood in the water,' one political activist ominously warned the website Politico, suggesting that voters would desert Biden en masse. Whilst polit-ical science professor and former Democratic strate-gist, Bob Shrum, told the Guardian, 'For him to recover from this would be a political miracle unlike anything we've seen in modern presidential politics . . .'

Fast-forward 3 weeks. A beaming Joe Biden bounced onto the stage in Los Angeles, flanked by his sister Valerie and wife, Jill[2]. 'They don't call it Super Tuesday for nothing!' he announced to a roar of approval from the cheering crowd, referring to the day on which voters in 14 states had just selected their chosen candidate for President. Incredibly, Joe Biden, on the canvas and being counted out in February, had burst back into contention with a series of devastating blows, winning 10 out of the 14 states on offer, including a clean sweep of the South and victory in Elizabeth Warren's home state of Massachusetts.

Elderly billionaire challenger, Mike Bloomberg, threw in the towel and joined Pete Buttigieg, plus a host of other young pretenders, to fall in line behind Joe Biden as the contender with the best chance of knocking out Trump. Only Bernie Sanders, the 'democratic socialist' senator from Vermont, remained a credible challenger for the nomination, and even he found himself slipping from being the favourite a few days earlier to suddenly trailing the resurgent former vice president.

When history tells the tale of Biden's comeback, the key moment may be seen to be a whispered conversation at a funeral in a South Carolina church, hundreds of miles away from the candidate himself. The conversation was initiated by an elderly African American lady with the words, 'Young man, I want you to whisper in my ear who you are voting for . . . I've been waiting to hear from you, this community needs to hear from you.' The 'young man' in question was 79-year-old James Clyburn, the veteran and highly influential South Carolina Congressman who is currently the highest-ranking African American in the Democratic Party.

The conversation spurred Clyburn into making a public and very heartfelt endorsement. 'I can think of no one better suited, better prepared ... no one with the integrity, no one more committed to the fundamental principles that make this country what it is than my good friend', said Clyburn at a joint event with Biden in North Charleston. With Clyburn's endorsement, Biden went from polling a narrow lead in South Carolina to sweeping the state with nearly 30% more of the vote than his nearest rival, Sanders. Significantly over 60% of African American voters, many inspired by Clyburn, swung behind Biden.

Biden's push for the presidency had been struggling with funding and underwhelming debate performances, but suddenly, after South Carolina, it had that most elusive and precious quality of any political campaign—momentum, or as the Biden team quickly rebranded it, 'Joe-mentum'. From down and seemingly out in New Hampshire, South Carolina helped Joe Biden back on his feet and set him up to deliver his knockout performance on Super Tuesday. 'To those who've [been] knocked down, counted out, left behind, this is your campaign,' declared a triumphant Biden from the stage in Los Angeles. ABC News called it 'a primary comeback beyond any that has come before.'

Seasoned watchers of Biden, however, would hardly have been surprised. Over the course of his long career, he's bounced back from ridiculous gaffes, humiliating scandals, political defeats, unimaginable personal tragedy, and being read the last rites. Even a political rival, Republican Leader of the Senate, Mitch McConnell, has paid warm tribute to Biden's incredible capacity to continue through the worst that life could throw at him. '[Joe] would be the first to tell you that he has been blessed in many ways. He has also been tested, knocked down, pushed to the edge of what anyone could be expected to bear, but from the grip of unknowable despair came a new man—a better man.'

If his latest—and probably final—campaign ends with him becoming, at 77, the oldest man ever elected as America's president, then it would surely be his most triumphant comeback of all. This is the story of the remarkable life of the man who just might become the 46th President of the United States . . .

'THE MEASURE OF A MAN . . .'
JOE BIDEN'S BIRTH AND ROOTS

November 1942—the world was at war. In Russia, the largest and bloodiest battle in the history of warfare was raging at Stalingrad. It would claim nearly two million casualties before it was done. In Egypt, success at El-Alamain stirred the morale of the Allied army after a year of setbacks and defeats. In the South Pacific, the naval forces of the USA and the Empire of Japan clashed in the Guadalcanal campaign, described by President Franklin D. Roosevelt as 'the turning point in this war'. Meanwhile, off the coast of North Africa, American warships triumphed in the naval battle of Casablanca, steadily tightening the noose that would eventually choke the Nazi forces occupying Europe.

In that same month, the movie "Casablanca", encouraging Americans to back the war effort, was premiered in New York. It would go on to be thought of as one of the greatest films of all time. Also in New York in November 1942 was a newly-born baby who would go on to be thought of as one of the greatest film directors of all time: Martin Scorsese. At the same time in Alabama, a US soldier named Al Hendrix was locked in a stockade to prevent him from sneaking off to Seattle to meet his newly-born son, Johnny, later known to the world as Jimi.

Another new baby who entered the world in that tumultuous month was Joseph Robinette Biden Jr, born in the town of Scranton, Pennsylvania on the morning of the 20th November 1942. He was the first child of Joseph Robinette Biden Sr and his wife, Catherine (née Finnegan).

As his mother's maiden name suggests, baby Biden had a strong dose of Irish blood in him. His family tree has been traced back to his maternal great-great-great-grandfather, Edward Blewitt, who was born in the final decade of the 18th century in the parish of Ballina in County Mayo on Ireland's wild Atlantic coast. Ballina has been home to notable revolutionaries and politicians, including independent Ireland's 7th President, Mary Robinson. Remarkably, Ballina is twinned with Scranton, where Biden himself was born.

Edward Blewitt was still living in Ballina when it became one of the worst struck areas during Ireland's 'Great Hunger' (the devastating potato famine of the 1840s). He was employed during the famine as an overseer at the Ballina workhouse, a government facility intended to provide support for the poor, which was soon overwhelmed by demand from starving locals. His public service during the famine has been praised by Irish historian, Ciarán Reilly, as having 'saved many lives'. But despite the efforts of Edward Blewitt and others, County Mayo lost 30% of its population to famine and emigration during the

Great Hunger and its aftermath. Many crossed the Atlantic on the so-called 'coffin ships', notorious for their horrific conditions and high mortality rates.

One of the young men who left the country at this time was Edward's young son, Patrick (Joe Biden's great-great-grandfather). Patrick was a rebel and trail-blazer. His eventual obituary in the Scranton Tribune said of him, 'Probably no Scranton man has ever lived a life so fraught with varied activities, romance and results.' Although, curiously, his travels and adventures began with him fleeing wedlock rather than famine. His father wanted to fix him up with a local girl in Ballina, but so resistant was the rebellious young Edward to the marriage that he fled to Liverpool, the main English port for Irish emigration, where he found employment as a cabin boy and escaped to the sea.

Undeterred by a fire that destroyed the first ship he sailed on, Patrick immediately returned to Liverpool, signed up on a second ship, and set off on a journey that eventually took him to Chile. There, by an incred-ible coincidence, he met and befriended a relative of the girl he'd run away from in Ballina. This man had made a fortune in his new home and offered to adopt young Patrick Blewitt as his son, but for a second time, he resisted the offer to join that family. Soon, the adventurous Patrick was off at sea again on a journey that would take him to Hawaii, China, and Japan, before finally landing in New York in 1851 at the age of just 18.

In America, he was reunited with his father, who had also joined the exodus from Ireland and was working as a pioneering surveyor in Pennsylvania, assisting Colonel Scranton with the laying out of the town that would bear his name. Patrick stopped sailing but continued to have an adventurous career, opening the first coal mine in Iowa, building railroads into the Brazilian jungle, and serving as a surveyor and mine inspector in Pennsylvania. He also took public office, serving as the head of the school board in Scranton.

In amongst all his adventures, Patrick found the time to get married to Catherine Scanlon in 1857, and to father 13 children. His son, Edward F. Blewitt (Biden's great-grandfather), worked as the city engineer for Scranton and also set a precedent for political success in the family by being elected to the state senate of Pennsylvania as a Democrat in 1907 (although his tenure only lasted two years). Edward was one of the first Roman Catholics elected to the state's senate, and no doubt would have been delighted if he could have known that his great-grandson would go on to become the first of that faith to hold the office of vice president of the United States.

Other Irish ancestors from Biden's mother's side, the Finnegans and Kearneys, were seaweed harvesters from County Louth on Ireland's east coast. Interestingly, Barack Obama's heritage has also been traced back to a family of Kearneys, although from a different part of Ireland. Biden's great-great-grandfather, Owen Finnegan, also moved to the US in the wake of the Irish famine, settling in the town of Ovid, New York during the 1850s. There, he worked as a boot and shoemaker, and had to make English his primary language for the first time. Owen's son, James, moved to Pennsylvania, and it was there that his son, Ambrose, married Geraldine, the daughter of Senator

Edward F. Blewitt—and this couple became Joe Biden's maternal grandparents.

Biden's father's family has been traced back to an Englishman from Sussex, William Biden, who was born around the same time as Edward Blewitt and who died in Baltimore in the 1840s. Elsewhere on that side of the family, there were more Irish and even French ancestors, which explains Biden's unusual middle name, Robinette[1]. According to family folklore, the Robinettes, Joe Biden's grandmother's family, crossed the Atlantic with Lafayette, the young Frenchman who served as a General in the American army during the War of Independence, and never returned.

Biden's paternal grandfather, Joseph H. Biden, was from Baltimore and worked as a salesman in the oil industry. Together with his wife Mary (née Robinette), and son Joseph, he moved to Scranton in the 1930s. It was there that Joseph Robinette Biden Sr. met Catherine Finnegan, known as Jean, and they married in 1941. The new Mr and Mrs Biden moved in with her parents on North Washington Street, and it was into this appropriately-named street that the baby who would come to dedicate his life to Washington was born on 20th November 1942.

At the time of Joe Biden's birth, his father was working for his rich uncle, Bill Sheen, whose company, Sheen Armor, made watertight sealants for merchant ships, a booming business during World War II. The demands of work meant he was not at home when his first child was born, but the house Biden was born into was full of family, with his mother, his maternal grandparents, his aunt Gertie, and his uncle Edward all living together. Uncle

Edward was known as Boo-Boo because of the stutter that impeded his attempts to pronounce his middle name (Blewitt), an affliction that would later play a defining role in the early life of the young Joe Biden.

Being born into a busy house in the working-class Green Ridge suburb of Scranton fits well with the popular image of Biden, having risen from humble beginnings, but the truth is a little bit more complicated. The wartime success of the Sheen Armor company meant that Biden's father was managing an office in Boston, driving a fancy Buick roadster convertible, and even flying off with his cousin in a private plane to hunt elk and bear in the Adirondack Mountains of upstate New York.

With the end of the war, however, the company's success came crashing down, and with it the fortunes of Joseph Biden Sr. He returned to Scranton and tried to get several businesses off the ground, including a furniture store and a crop-dusting enterprise, but none of them soared. Biden Sr was back to living with his in-laws. Generally, the joint family arrangement worked, with just the occasional tension rooted in the Biden and Finnegan families' different heritages from across the Atlantic. 'Your father is not a bad man,' Joe Biden remembers his auntie Gertie saying, 'he's just English.'

The already busy Biden household became even more crowded with the addition of his three siblings, Valerie, James, and Frank. The four young Bidens were incredibly close and unified, and stayed so throughout their lives, with Valerie growing up to work as Joe's campaign manager. Biden's interest in politics was fostered early in his household. Under the influence of his grandfather Ambrose and uncle Boo-Boo, he absorbed the dominant identity of Green Ridge from an early age, which was 'to be Irish, to be Democrat, to be Catholic, and there was no light between the three'.

The lessons Biden learned around the kitchen table in the Finnegan household would stand him in good stead for everything his tumultuous life would later throw at him. 'Champ,' his dad would tell him, 'the measure of a man is not how often he is knocked down, but how quickly he gets up.' Whilst his mother instilled in him a fierce egalitarianism. 'Remember, Joey,' she'd say, 'you're a Biden. Nobody is better than you. You're not better than anyone else, but *nobody* is better than you.' Years later, when Biden was due to travel for an audience with the Queen of the United Kingdom, his mother told him, 'Don't you bow down to her.'

Outside of the home, the young Biden demonstrated an aptitude for athletics and feats of daring that impressed his childhood friends. One story relates how he climbed one of Scranton's towering and unstable pyramids of smouldering coal debris to win a $5 bet (later putting the framed bill on the wall of his senate office). His 2020 election campaign adverts trade heavily on how 'the kid from Scranton' learned in his hometown about 'patriotism, friendship and faith'.

Biden's ancestors, both English and Irish, had been attracted to Scranton as a town whose success was fuelled by the coal-mining industry. But it was this very industry that went into terminal decline in Biden's childhood in the 1950s. Amongst the waves of people leaving Scranton for work elsewhere were the Bidens. In 1953, Joe Biden's dad found a job 140 miles away cleaning boilers. It was a considerable fall from grace from his days of private planes, but it was a job, at least. So, it was then that the Bidens uprooted and headed into the state that Joe would later come to represent for 36 years in the US senate—Delaware.

Donald Trump has tried to make political capital out of the departure of the 10-year-old Biden from Scranton, telling a rally in Pennsylvania in May 2019, 'Don't forget Biden deserted you. He's not from Pennsylvania. I guess he was born here, but he left you, folks. He left you for another state . . . This guy talks about oh, I know, Scranton . . . Well, I know the places better. He left you for another state and he didn't take care of you because he didn't take care of your jobs.'

The people of Scranton don't seem to agree. 'We love him', said Tom Owens, the current owner of the corner store where the young Biden used to buy his candy, which is now decorated with a life-size cut-out of the presidential hopeful. 'He's an honest guy, the kind of guy you respect, which we seem to be lacking a little bit in our leadership now. He's down to earth. I think he'd be a great president.' Jean W. Harris, a political scientist at the University of Scranton, confirmed Biden's popularity in his hometown, saying, 'Scrantonians see Biden as one of their own . . . [he] is certainly viewed [here] as a hard-working, blue-collar-aligned Pennsylvanian.'

Biden's popularity in Scranton might help to explain why the crucial Rust Belt swing state strongly backed his running mate, Barack Obama, in 2008 and 2012[2]. In 2012, Lackawanna, the county where Scranton resides, voted for the Obama-Biden ticket by a majority of 27%. When given the choice between Hillary Clinton and Donald Trump in the presidential election of 2016, the state of Pennsylvania narrowly voted for the Republican.

It is understandable that Trump is keen to use any means he can to undermine Biden in a key state, but his accusations hardly seem fair. The young Joe Biden might have been taken out of Scranton, but his hometown never left him. He continued to return frequently with his family and never lost touch with his childhood friends, even when his stellar political career took off[3]. Buddies from his youth were invited to all significant events in Biden's life, including his taking of the vice-presidential oath of office on Inauguration Day in 2009.

Looking back, they claimed to be unsurprised that their daring little pal went on to achieve international renown. 'We weren't thinking it was at all odd that Joe Biden achieved greatness in life', remembered his old friend, Tommy Bell. 'We just assumed it would happen, whatever it was going to be . . .'

2

'HE'S GOING TO BE PRESIDENT OF THE UNITED STATES!' BIDEN'S POLITICAL AWAKENING IN THE '50S AND '60S

Biden's closest friends from Scranton might have always foreseen his rise to prominence, but most of the other people he came into contact with from his childhood almost certainly didn't. There was a reason for this. Just like uncle Boo-Boo, the young Joe was afflicted by a stutter that seemed likely to restrict his prospects. It was so bad that he was exempted from public speaking assignments at high school, and the scars it left on him obviously ran deep; the first chapter of Biden's autobiography is entitled 'Impedimenta' after the cruel high school nickname his stutter earned him.

Poor old Boo-Boo blamed his stutter for the fact he never married, and gave it as the reason why, despite his brains, he'd never become a doctor but instead had ended up as a travelling salesman for a mattress company. Biden's stutter might have seemed to pose similar problems, but instead, it became the first of the many challenges that he overcame—setting a precedent for the rest of his life and the bigger struggles to come. As Biden himself put it, 'that impedimenta ended up being a godsend for me. Carrying it strengthened me . . . and the very things it taught me turned out to be invaluable lessons for my life as well as my chosen career.'

The stutter wasn't always a problem for Biden, being largely under control back in the Finnegan house in Scranton, or when he was with his close friends. But change and new challenges seemed to bring it out, and in that context, the move to Delaware and starting at a few new schools in quick succession must have been a particularly tough time for the young Joe Biden.

Rapid change was also prevalent in 1950s America. In the time between the end of the war and Biden's 18th birthday in 1960, the country's GDP more than doubled, and with all the extra wealth came sprawling suburbs—including the Bidens' new place on the edge of Wilmington—housing people who were escaping the cities in search of a suburban American dream. At the same time, these homes were being filled with new consumer goods like television sets, with 77% of American households getting their first TV during the 1950s.

From these TV sets and old radios blared the new sounds of a youth culture, epitomised by the rock 'n' roll which electrified the America of Biden's formative years. He was 12 years old when Bill Haley's exhortation to the youth of America to 'Rock Around the Clock' hit the top of the charts and inspired rioting in cinemas across the land, and 13 when Elvis Presley took his famous trip down Lonely Street to 'Heartbreak Hotel'.

Along with the rapid cultural change came the new

world of the 'cold war' to adjust to, and new challenges to the old establishment, particularly with the civil rights struggle against entrenched racism across America. The 1954 Brown v. Board of Education case rendered the racial segregation of children in public schools illegal, and set in motion a chain of events that would cause a controversy that dogs Biden's political career to this day.

By his own admission, Biden was never heavily involved in the civil rights struggles that spread across America in the '50s and '60s, although he did once join a sit-in against a segregated cinema, and also possibly led a walkout from a diner that refused service to the only black member of his high school football team. He also worked a summer job when he was 19 as the only white lifeguard at a swimming pool serving a black housing project. 'It was the first time', Biden later recalled, 'that I got to know well and become good friends with all these inner-city black guys . . . it was a great awakening for me . . . in my neighbourhood there were no African Americans . . . you didn't know how people were being treated.'

Biden was an average student academically, but one area he did excel at in school was in sports, specifically American football. His high school coach, John Walsh, described him as 'the most talented receiver I ever had.' When Walsh took over the team at Archmere Academy, they had a terrible record of only ten wins in the previous twelve years. But with Walsh's coaching and the contributions of his star player, the team went on to win every game in Biden's senior year at the school. Their triumphant season ended with Biden scoring a touchdown in the last minute of the final game. His coach and teammates remember Biden for being highly competitive, highly confident, and never troublesome.

His sporting prowess undoubtedly earned Biden a status amongst his peers that would not normally be afforded to a pupil struggling with a debilitating stutter. But as well as winning respect on the sporting field, he also put in the hours required to overcome his speech impediment altogether. Biden tried various methods to defeat his stutter, from speech therapy to filling his mouth with pebbles in imitation of the celebrated Greek orator, Demosthenes, who suffered from the same problem. The Demosthenes trick didn't work, but hours spent alone in front of the mirror practising elocution did. By the time of his high school graduation ceremony, Biden was able to deliver the welcome address without a single stutter.

His tongue liberated, Biden has barely stopped talking since, and has built a career on his words; although many times he's talked himself into all sorts of trouble, too. Overcoming his stutter was an essential step in his rise to prominence, but having the stutter in the first place was equally important in forming his character and helping him to succeed. According to his sister, Valerie, it encouraged in him a compassionate and inclusive spirit, 'because he knew what it feels like to be laughed at . . . so he always attempted to bring people in.'

His stutter conquered, the young Biden was able to plan for his future with renewed confidence. As a 17-year-old, he'd long since forgotten an earlier ambition to become a priest, and took inspiration instead from the rise of a charismatic young Democratic politician whose pursuit of the presidency brought him national, and subsequently global, fame.

John Fitzgerald Kennedy was a Harvard graduate from a very wealthy and politically well-connected Bostonian family. His grandfather was a congressman and twice mayor of Boston, and his father a highly successful businessman who also served as the American ambassador to the UK. The contrast with Biden's father, by this time a used car salesman, could hardly have been greater. However, both JFK and Biden shared a common Irish American heritage and a Catholic faith, and in the America of the early 1960s, that was a big deal indeed.

The historian Arthur M. Schlesinger Sr called anti-Catholicism 'The biggest bias in the history of the American people', which is a bold claim in a country still struggling with the legacy of slavery. Anti-Catholicism was, however, one of the explicit aims of the resurgent Ku Klux Klan of the 20th century (which reached an estimated peak of up to 4 million members in the 1920s). It was also a significant issue in the 1928 election—the only previous occasion when one of the major parties had fielded a Catholic candidate[1]. In 1960, the year of Kennedy's presidential campaign, Pulitzer prize-winning poet and professor Peter Viereck called Catholic baiting 'the anti-Semitism of the liberals'. Prejudice was mixed up with a fear that electing a Catholic would give the Pope undue influence over American affairs.

Nevertheless, Kennedy overcame any bias against his background and faith to become the first—and to date, only—Catholic President of the United States, achieving a stunning victory over Richard Nixon. The 1960 election (held 12 days before Biden's 18th birthday) was the closest in 20th century America in terms of the popular vote, with Kennedy winning only

112,000 more people than Nixon across a nation in which nearly 69 million people voted[2].

Kennedy was perhaps boosted by nuns in Catholic schools around the world, like those teaching Biden at Archmere Academy, who implored their pupils to pray for the success of their co-religionist in his pursuit of the presidency. The nuns might have been less enthused for Kennedy had they have known about his predilection for extra-marital affairs, which came to light only after his assassination.

Nevertheless, in 1960, scandal seemed far from the golden boy of American politics. At 43, Kennedy was the youngest president ever elected, and he was helping to inspire a new generation of young Americans, including Joe Biden, to go into politics. 'I was swept up', Biden would later say of the great leaders of the 1960s like the Kennedy brothers, 'in their eloquence, their conviction, the sheer size of their impossible dreams.'

Biden was, however, realistic enough to recognise that following in Kennedy's footsteps would not be easy for someone from a humbler background. He was also smart enough to pick up the Congressional Directory in his school library and skim through the biographical details of the senators, spotting that many of them had pursued careers in law prior to politics. So, it was in the autumn of 1961 that Biden came to enrol at the University of Delaware, majoring in political science and history, with a plan to go on to law school and a career in politics.

Biden soon enjoyed electoral success at university, becoming president of his first-year class. He was a popular, clean-cut figure who didn't drink or smoke. 'We didn't even know what marijuana was', recalled an old classmate from that time. Biden has been a life-long teetotaller after having seen the effects of alco-holism in his own family. Whilst at university, he was noted for his smart dress sense and for dating a string of good-looking girls, although, on one occasion, the clean-living Biden ended the date early because the girl lit a cigarette. The only trouble Biden seems to have got into at university was a few run-ins with the campus police when he was caught in the vicinity of the women's dormitory.

While on a spring break trip to the Bahamas in 1964, the 21-year-old Biden started dating the girl who would transform him from a serial monogamist into a happily married man, Neilia Hunter. He met her after sneaking into the expensive place where she was staying and stealing a hotel towel to pretend he was a guest too. With a typically colourful turn of phrase, Biden described himself as having fallen 'ass over tin cup in love at first sight.' Neilia was equally smitten; her friend, Bobbie Greene, remembers her reporting back on her new boyfriend, 'Do you know what he's going to be? He's going to be a senator by age 30, and he's going to be President of the United States!' Her first prediction came true, and the second might still.

Biden's initial brief encounter with Neilia changed his life forever, in the short-term leading him to study at Syracuse Law School, New York (so he could be close to her), and ultimately, to the tragedy that would nearly destroy him.

3

'A COAT AND TIE GUY WHO WOULD DO EVERYTHING CORRECTLY . . .' BIDEN'S PATH INTO POLITICS

Between Biden starting at Delaware University in autumn 1961 and enrolling at Syracuse Law School in spring 1965, the America around him had changed radically. Kennedy was dead, assassinated in Dallas on 22nd November 1963, two days after Biden's 21st birthday. 'When he died,' commented US Ambassador Brandon Grove, 'so, once again, did American innocence and a large piece of our native optimism . . . as individuals we seem to have shorter time for being young.'

In retrospect, the Kennedy era was not so carefree as it may have appeared. His presidency had seen the world brought to the precipice of nuclear conflict with the Cuban Missile Crisis, and an upsurge in American military involvement in Vietnam would lead to the first US combat troops entering the war there from March 1965.

Kennedy also presided over dramatic developments in space exploration, with the first American astronaut taking off in 1961, and a commitment to reaching the moon before the decade was out. On the domestic front, he proposed civil rights legislation, which, like engagement in Vietnam, would only come to fruition under his successor, Lyndon B. Johnson.

The Cultural Revolution was also taking place in the America of the early 1960s. The landmark moment for this was the Beatles' legendary appearance on the Ed Sullivan Show in February 1964, with a performance which has been credited with shaking America out of the national depression it had fallen into following Kennedy's assassination three months earlier. By the time Biden was starting at law school, the Beatles were already well on their way with the transformation that would take them from be-suited rock 'n' roll revivalists who wanted to hold your hand, to beard-sprouting gurus claiming to be walruses.

No such changes were going on with the young Joe Biden, who remained, according to Neilia's friend Bobbie, 'a very straight arrow.' His love for Neilia might have redirected him to Syracuse, but he was still the same sporty, clean-cut, confident, politically-focused, and academically average student he'd always been. Biden had struggled to get the grades necessary at Delaware to go to law school, but inspired by Neilia, he stepped up his efforts in his final year sufficiently to be rewarded with a place at Syracuse (still ranking only an unimpressive 506th out of 688 in his class).

Whilst at Syracuse, his familiar problems of under-application and academic under-achievement reappeared, this time with some added complications. During his first term, another student, apparently jealous of Biden's popularity on campus, reported him for plagiarism in one of his papers. Biden, who claimed he was just ignorant of how to properly cite other people's work, was summoned before the deans and ordered to repeat the course. Biden resubmitted and passed, and the incident appeared to be quickly dead and buried, but it resurfaced 23 years later at a most embarrassing time for a man then running for the highest office in the land.

Biden also got an early taste of electoral defeat whilst at Syracuse, losing a bid to be first-year class president by a single vote to a well-connected New Yorker named Bill Brodsky. At the time of writing, it remains to be seen whether this will be an omen for a forthcoming presidential struggle with another New Yorker scheduled for November 2020.

Despite these various setbacks, Biden's life generally went extremely well in Syracuse. He continued to be, in the words of his professor James K. Weeks in 1967, 'Far from distinguished scholastically . . . but he knows what he is doing and appears to possess good judgement and a highly developed sense of responsibility. He is the type of individual one is more than willing to take a chance on, because he is unlikely to sell short your expectations.'

Another professor, Thomas Maroney, later remembered thinking Biden 'might not wind up being the top student in his class but he was going to wind up as somebody someday. He had a natural bent, a presence.' Ironically, Biden's previous weakest point, public speaking, had turned into his greatest strength. Long hours spent reciting memorised passages before the mirror helped him to speak confidently without notes, engaging the audience as he talked and tailoring his speech in response to their reactions.

Biden married Neilia at the end of his first year at law school, and they moved into a house in Syracuse while he finished his studies (ranking 76th of the 85 students in his class at graduation) and she began teaching at a local elementary school. After graduation, the couple had to decide between remaining in New York state or returning to Delaware, where Biden had grown up. A contact of his father's persuaded him that Delaware, the second smallest and most corporate-dominated[1] state in the US, was the best place to practice law in the country and helped Biden to find work at the firm of Prickett, Ward, Burt, & Sanders.

The Bidens moved back to Wilmington, and it was there that their first son, officially Joseph Robinette Biden III, but always known as Beau, was born in February 1969. He was followed soon after by another son, Robert Hunter Biden, known as Hunter, in February 1970. At the time Hunter was born, his father was stretching out his income from his job at the law firm by also working as a maintenance man and lifeguard at the pool of a country club, a job which came with rent-free accommodation in a cottage on the grounds.

Wilmington, around that time, had been making national headlines for the scale of its crackdown against the civil rights protests and race riots that had flared up in the city following the assassination of Martin Luther King in Memphis on 4th April 1968. The Democratic Governor of Delaware, Charles Terry, ordered the National Guard onto the streets of Wilmington and kept them there until January of the following year. Not since the Civil War of a century earlier had such a lengthy military deployment been seen on American streets. Biden was so opposed to Terry's handling of the situation that he went against

his own upbringing and voted for the Republican
candidate in the 1968 gubernatorial election.

Biden himself was not, however, an active civil
rights protester; he was 'more of a system person than
working outside the system', said Ted Kaufman, his
advisor and later successor in the Senate. 'He wore a
sport jacket, not a flak jacket.' He also did not become
directly involved in the anti-war protests sweeping the
nation, even though he came to oppose US involvement in Vietnam. 'He was a coat and tie guy', one
friend from the period remembered, 'and would do
everything correctly.'

Biden also avoided the fate of over 2 million of his
contemporaries who were drafted into the US army at
the time of Vietnam. As a student during the early
years of the war, he was eligible for draft deferments
on five occasions. When his studies were subsequently
completed, records released in 2008 showed that he
was not conscripted because he had suffered from
asthma as a teenager. Strangely, he makes no mention
of this asthma in his autobiography, and it seems
slightly at odds with his own accounts of a highly
sporting childhood.

Although Biden was not an active protester
throughout this period, he was prepared to take a
stand on a matter of principle, even to the detriment
of his own career. In 1969, the firm for which Biden
worked was involved in the defence of a company
being sued by one of their members of staff for negli-
gence which had resulted in the worker being severely
burned and permanently disabled. Biden was part of
the team that helped the company win its case, but in
the immediate aftermath of the verdict, he felt sufficiently distressed that he lied to the senior partner

from his firm in order to avoid having to go for lunch for him. 'It's the only time I can ever remember lying', recalled Biden, a claim which, if true, suggests he might be the most forgetful lawyer and politician in history.

Recognising that he was on the wrong path, Biden quit his job and presented himself at the Office of the Public Defender, looking for a new role that more closely matched his ethics. In his new post, 90% of his clients were African Americans from disadvantaged neighbourhoods. This period of Biden's life also saw him start to become more actively engaged in politics. Registering as a Democrat in 1969, he became involved with progressive local members who hoped to modernise the party away from the sort of repressive racial policies epitomised by Governor Terry's military occupation of Wilmington. The history of the Democratic Party, it is worth remembering, was one particularly stained by racial prejudice; after all, it had been Abraham Lincoln's Republicans who had ended slavery in the face of the opposition of many Democrats.

Biden was soon identified as a rising star in the local Democratic Party, and at the age of just 27, he was offered the opportunity to run for a seat on the New Castle County Council. Initially reluctant, as his focus was more on federal—and indeed, international —political affairs, Biden was won over by the pragmatic argument that he had to start somewhere. The seat in question was in a traditionally Republican district, but Biden, heavily supported by his three siblings, especially his sister Valerie, set to work with great gusto. Between them, the four Bidens knocked on every door in the district and came up with a powerful campaign focused on residents' concerns about crime, refuse collection, and urban over-development.

On an otherwise disastrous election night for the Democrats in Delaware, Biden took the County Council seat from the Republicans by over 2,000 votes. The year was 1970, and Biden had taken his first significant step towards achieving his political ambitions. Almost immediately, he turned his attention to the great leap he hoped to make next—into the US Senate. But in his way stood perhaps the most formidable obstacle in Delaware's political history.

4

'I WILL NEVER AGAIN THINK OF SOMETHING AS IMPOSSIBLE . . .' THE SENATE CAMPAIGN OF 1972

By 1972, Republican Senator James Caleb ('Cale') Boggs was a giant of the Delaware political scene. Boggs was a locally born and bred veteran of WWII with nearly thirty years of governmental service experience behind him. When Biden was just three years old, Boggs had been elected as Delaware's sole member of the House of Representatives. He won re-election twice and only left the house after winning the race to become the tiny state's governor in 1952, the year in which a 10-year-old Biden arrived from Pennsylvania. Again, he won re-election in that role, and only left the post for a further step up, taking a seat in the US Senate in 1960 (the only Republican to defeat a Democratic incumbent in the year of Kennedy's election).

By 1972, Boggs had a track record of over a quarter century of major electoral success in Delaware. In contrast, Joe Biden was an academically undistinguished 29-year-old lawyer, with just one local election victory and two years' experience on the County

Council to his name. While Boggs debated the great issues of state in the Senate, Biden was still doubling up as a part-time pool attendant at a local country club. But if he wanted to achieve his ambition of breaking through to the national political scene, Boggs was the man he would have to overcome.

Even though he was technically too young to take a Senate seat at the time of the election, winning the Democratic nomination to stand in the election was the easy part for Biden[1], for the simple reason that no one else wanted it. Boggs was considered too tough to take on. The Wilmington Journal referred to Biden as a 'sacrificial lamb'.

However, what no-one in the Democratic Party truly appreciated at the time was that the old veteran, Boggs, was weary and lacking the heart to enter into another electoral battle. Initially reluctant to defend his seat at all, he only relented under considerable pressure from both the local Republican Party and President Richard Nixon[2], and, like an old prize-fighter, stepped into the ring one final time.

Perhaps it was this reluctance, combined with overconfidence in the face of his novice challenger, that explained why Boggs ran such a lacklustre campaign. Despite having access to far greater finan-cial resources than his opponent, Boggs had, by mid-September (less than two months before the election date), only spent a miserly $3,000 on his campaign, compared to a $50,000 spend by Biden.

Biden's campaign was also characterised by a youthful energy completely lacking from his oppo-nent's corner. While Boggs slumbered peacefully, Biden was launching his push for the Senate to a crowded and somewhat sceptical room at the Hotel

Du Pont, after which he co-piloted a light aircraft over the state, his young son Beau on his lap.

All of Biden's family featured very heavily in his campaign, which was led by his sister Valerie, criss-crossing the tiny state on a mission to shake hands and drink coffee with every single Delawarean. So engrossed were the whole Biden family, including his wife, Neilia, in the election, that no one was left to look after his young children, so Beau, Hunter, and their new baby sister, Naomi were loaded up in wicker baskets and carried door-to-door on the campaign trail[3].

At the heart of it all was Biden himself. 'He was like the Energiser Bunny', recalled Rich Heffron, one of his campaign team. 'He'd never stop. If you went to a high school football game on Saturday morning, he was there. If you went to the Acme, he was there. If you went to the Delaware football game in the afternoon, he was there. He would go to those polka dances in the old Polish section of town. He'd shake hands. He had that smile, that grin; he was everybody's best friend.'

The efforts of Biden and his family were supplemented by those of a mass of eager youthful supporters, enthused by the handsome young candidate offering a fresh face for their state. Jane Harriman, a reporter at the Wilmington Journal, compared them to 'Beatlemaniacs' and spotted in Biden the potential to be 'Delaware's JFK'. Biden also had the added advantage of youthful good looks. 'The girls think he's sexy and say so with little provocation', reported journalist Norm Lockman shortly before the election.

Biden appealed to a broad spectrum of young voters and was highly successful at getting them actively engaged. 'It seemed', recalled David Topel, one of Biden's young volunteers, 'more like a movement than a campaign, an opportunity to have our voices heard in a wartime atmosphere that had set the generations at odds.' The parallels with the current presidential campaign of Biden's rival for the Democratic nomination, Bernie Sanders, are striking. Although in '72, Biden's young volunteers were taking to their bikes to hand-deliver his self-printed weekly campaign newspapers (the pre-social media era equivalent of a Twitter account and a Facebook page).

Also, Biden was, even back then, very much the moderate relative to progressives like Sanders. His campaign priorities were, in his own words, 'Voting rights, civil rights, crime, clean water and clean air, pensioner protection, health care, and the war in Vietnam.' But on none of these issues did he take an overly radical stance. On civil rights, for example, he made it clear that he sided with his rival, Boggs, in his opposition to busing black children to predominantly white schools to combat segregation in Delaware, a policy position that continues to cause controversy[4].

By 1972, even opposition to the war had gone from being the preserve of beatniks and hippies to a mainstream issue, with the multi-million strong Vietnam Moratorium demonstrations of 1969, described by Pulitzer prize-winning journalist, Stanley Karnow, as 'a sober almost melancholy manifestation of middle class concern.' Biden won support from young voters for his vocal opposition to the conflict[5], contrasting himself to Boggs's record of voting in support of increased funding for the war effort, but maintained elements of moderation in his position, arguing against amnesty for 'draft-dodgers' who had fled the country to avoid conscription.

His core campaign message, as he described it looking back, was 'I still believed in the system, I wanted to make it work, and I could be trusted to try.' In keeping with this moderation, his campaign against Boggs was characterised by a level of decorum that seems quite quaint when compared to the ferocious mud-slinging, and worse, of modern politics. Both candidates found common ground in their debates, and Biden was keen to show his respect for the elder statesman. 'I don't think [anybody] can find anything unethical about Senator Boggs,' he said, 'he's just a very ethical guy.' Boggs reciprocated with words of personal praise for Biden, telling reporters, 'I like him very much.'

Biden even took to wearing one of his rivals' 'I love Cale' badges inside his jacket and showed it to any die-hard Boggs supporters he encountered on his constant campaign tour. Biden's approach may have been born out of his own 1950s values, but it was also a wise piece of political calculation. Boggs was enormously popular in Delaware, and the so-called 'first state' was proud of its civility. Any attempt to import firebrand politics would only have exploded in Biden's face. Following the announcement of the result, the two candidates even shared a ride in a horse-drawn carriage—a Delaware tradition.

As the campaign went on, Biden's hard work, well-chosen policy positions and effective advertising saw him creeping up in the polls. Slowly, it dawned on the Boggs campaign that the young challenger was a genuine contender, and they made a late effort to come out of their corner fighting. The knockout punch they readied themselves to release was a full-page advert in Delaware's leading Sunday newspaper two days before the election. By this time, the Biden campaign was all punched-out with no funds left to defend itself against the impact of Boggs's last-minute blow.

But then came a stroke of fortune that saved the day for Biden and ended up providing the basis on which his future career was built. There was a sudden newspaper strike immediately before the election, which meant that Boggs's final punch never landed, his expensive advert going unseen across the state.

Or was it good fortune? Intriguingly, the 2004 biography of Mafia hitman and trade unionist, Frank 'The Irishman' Sheeran, alleged that the strike was instigated by an unidentified lawyer in the Delaware Democratic Party in order to prevent Boggs' advert from going out. Sheeran, the subject of Martin Scorsese's acclaimed 2019 movie, 'The Irishman', was in charge of the local Teamsters Union in Wilmington at the time and claimed to have organised a picket line made up of 'people nobody would mess with.' He claimed that, after the strike, anytime he wanted to 'reach out to [Biden] he would listen.'

Sheeran's account has been called into question because of inconsistencies between his claims and the facts printed in the Wilmington News Journal around the time, not least the fact that it was a different union —not the Teamsters—who called and led the strike. The truth may never be known, but what is certain is that the strike stopped Boggs from responding to a couple of digs Biden had thrown into his final news-paper adverts, which had presented the old-timer as out of touch[6].

Who knows what difference it made to the final outcome? But when it came to the count on 7th

November 1972, Biden, against all odds, triumphed by just under 3,000 votes (a majority of 1.4% of the vote). The margin was thin enough that the advert that never went out might have made the difference. Nevertheless, Biden had done it, becoming the second youngest man to be elected to the US Senate in history, despite an otherwise disastrous showing for the Democrats in the presidential election that took place on that same day[7]. His victory remains one of the most stunning upsets in US electoral history.

'I've been doing this for almost 50 years', reflected Biden's long-term aide and eventual senatorial successor, Ted Kaufmann, 'and people talk to me about campaigns: Senate campaigns, presidential campaigns, congressional campaigns, local representative campaigns. I have never seen a single one that can compare to the Biden '72 campaign in terms of the size of the upset.' After the election, Kaufman remembers resolving to himself, 'I will never again think of something as impossible.'

At 29, Biden had sent shockwaves through the political establishment of Delaware. But they were nothing compared to the shock that was about to rip apart his own life and take him from his moment of triumph to a scarcely imaginable personal hell.

5

'WE WERE ON TOP OF THE WORLD AND THEN THE WORLD ENDED . . .' THE CRASH

The day after Biden's election success, his baby daughter, Naomi, celebrated her first birthday. It would be hard to imagine two more delighted parents on that day. Neilia, age 30, had been the Senior Political Strategist on the campaign that had seen Joe, 29, elected to the senate. Together, they had pulled off one of the most sensational shocks in US electoral history.

It's easy to imagine how enthused Biden was about his baby daughter's birthday. Little Naomi, known as Amy (or Caspy after her resemblance to the cartoon character, Casper the Friendly Ghost), was the apple of her dad's eye. 'The only good thing in the world is kids', Biden had told Jane Harriman in an interview back in the days when he only had two boys, joking with her that he planned to 'keep [Neilia] pregnant until I have a little girl.'

Naomi's birth in 1971 had completed the family, and the Bidens planned to have no further children because of, Joe later recalled, a premonition that if they had another, something would go wrong. On her first birthday, while the family celebrated, Biden had another bad feeling, telling Neilia, 'It's too perfect. Can't be like this, something's gonna happen.'

On Monday 18th December 1972, one week before Christmas, Joe Biden set off from his home in Wilmington to catch a train to Washington, where he was busy finding a place to live and interviewing prospective staff members for his new team. He was not due to take up his seat in the Senate until 6th January 1973, so there was plenty of time to make all the arrangements before he started. Neilia had originally planned to accompany him, but changed her mind and stayed in Wilmington with the children to make preparations for what was surely going to be a super-special Christmas, with three children under 4 and a new senator in the family.

With Joe gone, she packed the kids, Beau, Hunter, and Naomi, into the car and set off on a shopping trip to Hockessin, a suburb of Wilmington, to buy the Christmas tree. Also on the streets of Hockessin that day was Curtis Dunn, who was driving a truck back to his home in Kaolin, just across the Pennsylvania-Delaware border.

At 2:30 in the afternoon, Neilia was heading for home and pulled out at a junction. Dunn's truck, which had been driving down a long hill, smashed straight into her car with such force that it travelled over 150 feet down the road before it fell backwards down an embankment and crashed into three trees. The truck itself spun over onto its side as Dunn tried to swerve out of the way. He then climbed out and ran to the car. Who can imagine the hell he found inside?

In an office in Washington where Joe Biden was working, a phone started to ring. It was his brother,

Jimmy, asking to speak to their sister, Val. She took the call and hung up shortly afterwards. 'There's been a slight accident, nothing to worry about. But we better go home.' Biden, according to his memoir, knew instantaneously what had happened. 'What I felt was something jarring, something stronger than a premonition. It was a physical sensation, like a little pinprick at the center of my chest. I could already feel Neilia's absence. "She's dead," I said, "isn't she?"'

The truth was even worse. Not only was Neilia dead, but baby Naomi had also been killed in the crash. Both had died before reaching the hospital. Whilst coping with the death of his wife, Biden would also have to bear for the first time the unimaginable pain of burying a child. It would not be the last. 'We were on top of the world on November 9', remembered Biden's sister Val, 'and then on December 18 the world ended.'

Biden's boys had survived the crash, but with serious injuries that kept them hospitalised for weeks. Three-year-old Beau had broken his leg and was required to wear a full-body cast. Two-year-old Hunter had suffered head injuries, including fracturing his skull. He has said repeatedly since that his earliest memory is of waking up in a hospital bed by the side of his brother, who turned to him and said, 'I love you, I love you, I love you.'

On at least two occasions, Biden has publicly suggested that Dunn was under the influence of alcohol at the wheel. He told a crowd at an event on the 2008 presidential campaign trail that his wife and daughter had been killed by 'a guy who allegedly—and I never pursued it—drank his lunch instead of eating his lunch.' But these claims are contradicted by the evidence of the blood tests taken after the accident, which showed that the driver had not been drinking. Biden contacted the daughter of the then-deceased Dunn in 2009 to apologise for his accusations.

Political opponents in the media have tried to make capital out of Biden's false version of events, using it to question his character. But grief counsellor Rob Zucker gave a more charitable interpretation, explaining that grieving people often retell their stories in ways which shift blame. 'It's a common challenge bereaved parents in particular struggle with after a sudden, violent death. I think the fact that [Biden] has this way of sometimes understanding the story is really an expression of the challenge for any person to go forward in their lives.'

The tragic truth appears to be that Neilia, in a car full of young children, simply made a single second mistake which ended up taking her own life and that of her daughter. Jerome O. Herlihy, who was the deputy attorney general of Delaware at the time, and a friend of Biden, said in a later interview, 'She had a stop sign. The truck driver did not.' The same source also said Neilia had baby Naomi on her lap at the time, which sounds terrible when viewed from a 21st-century perspective, but which would hardly have been deemed unusual in the America of 1972 (no state had legislation requiring children to be in car seats until Tennessee in 1979).

Imprisoned by despair, Biden considered suicide. 'The first few days,' he wrote in his memoir, 'I felt trapped in a constant twilight of vertigo, like in the dream where you're suddenly falling . . . only I was constantly falling . . . I began to understand how despair led people to just cash it in; how suicide wasn't just an option but a *rational* option. But I'd look at Beau and Hunter asleep and wonder what new terrors their own dreams held, and wonder who would explain to my sons my being gone, too. And I knew had no choice but to fight to stay alive.'

Seeking to escape from the grief that tormented him, Biden took to the streets, as he described in one of the most candid sections of his autobiography. 'When the boys were asleep or when Val or Mom was taking a turn at their bedside, I'd bust out of the hospital and go walking the nearby streets. Jimmy would go with me, and I'd steer him wordlessly down into the darkest and seediest neighborhoods I could find. I liked to go at night when I thought there was a better chance of finding a fight. I was always looking for a fight. I had not known I was capable of such rage. I knew I had been cheated out of a future, but I felt I'd been cheated of a past, too. The underpinnings of my life had been kicked out from under me . . . I felt God had played a horrible trick on me, and I was angry. I found no comfort in the Church. So I kept walking the dark streets to try to exhaust the rage.'

Of course, Biden's recent electoral triumph also seemed utterly hollow, and he resolved to not take the Senate seat he had won so he could focus on being with his boys. But eventually, both his family and fellow senators were able to persuade him that he should not give up that which he and Neilia had fought so hard for, that being a good father and a good senator were not incompatible and that work might help him to find a path through his grief.

So, on 5th January 1973, Biden twice took the oath of office of the US Senate from inside Beau's hospital bedroom. He took it twice because so many TV cameras were there to cover the story of the tragic young senator that they couldn't all cram in to film it the first time. When the oath was done, he addressed the watching nation, saying, 'I hope that I can be a good senator for you all. I make this one promise: if in six months time or so there's a conflict between my being a good father and being a good senator . . . I promise you I will contact Governor-elect Tribbitt[1] . . . and tell him we can always get another senator, but they [Beau and Hunter] can't get another father.'

If he had quit in that time frame, Biden's would have been one of the shortest tenures of any senator. As it came to be, thirty-five years after making that promise, Biden was still occupying his Senate seat.

6

'DEATH AND THE ALL-AMERICAN BOY . . .' BIDEN'S EARLY YEARS IN THE SENATE

In May 1974, the youngest senator in the USA was visited by reporter Kitty Kelley from the Washingtonian. Her subsequent portrait of him, published under the title 'Death and the All-American Boy', was an unusually candid and raw depiction of a politician still battling against deep waves of grief.

The portrait starts, inevitably, with Neilia. '[She] was my very best friend, my greatest ally, my sensuous lover. The longer we lived together the more we enjoyed everything from sex to sports. Most guys don't really know what I lost because they never knew what I had. Our marriage was sensational. It was exceptional, and now that I look around at my friends and my colleagues, I know more than ever how phenomenal it really was. When you lose something like that, you lose a part of yourself that you never get back again.'

Biden credited his dead wife with his electoral success, describing her as 'the brains behind my campaign . . . She was the most intelligent human

being I have ever known . . . At first she stayed at home
with the kids while I campaigned but that didn't work
out because I'd come back too tired to talk to her. I
might satisfy her in bed but I didn't have much time
for anything else. That's when she started campaigning
with me and that's when I started winning. You know,
the people of Delaware really elected her, but they
got me.'

Kelley counted over 35 pictures of Neilia on the
walls of Biden's office. He shared with her his
favourite one, adding, 'she had the best body of any
woman I ever saw. She looks better than a Playboy
bunny, doesn't she?' Also on his walls was a framed
copy of Milton's 'On His Deceased Wife', which
describes a dream-visit by the poet's late beloved: 'But
O as to embrace me she enclin'd / I wak'd, she fled, and
day brought back my night.' It was a poem that Biden
had quoted in his memorial address for Neilia, and
which contained a particularly poignant echo of
Biden's own circumstances, as Milton's wife had
passed away shortly after giving birth to a baby daughter, who had also died.

The talk turned to politics and the report revealed
a Joe Biden who was enjoying being the rising star of
the Senate, but very keen to distance himself from
what might be the expected policy positions of a
young man who came of age in the 1960s. 'When it
comes to civil rights and civil liberties, I'm a liberal but
that's it. I'm really quite conservative on most other
issues. My wife said I was the most socially conservative man she had ever known. I'm a screaming liberal
when it comes to senior citizens because I really think
they are getting screwed. I'm a liberal on health care
because I believe it is a birth right of every human

being . . . But when it comes to issues like abortion, amnesty, and acid, I'm about as liberal as your grandmother.'[1]

At the same time, he also explained his belief that issues don't matter when it comes to winning elections. Issues, claimed Biden, 'are merely a vehicle to portray your intellectual capacity to the voters . . . a vehicle by which the voters will determine your honesty and candor.' Kelley quotes a man who had witnessed a Biden speech who was both impressed by his honesty and suspicious that it was a product of political calculation, saying, 'I'm not sure he doesn't use candor as a calculated device. It's probably more deliberate than spontaneous. But it works. His performance is so professionally orchestrated it seems natural and sincere . . . and I must admit, compared to the rest of those tired old hacks on Capitol Hill, he is the best and brightest hope we have right now. I'd vote for him for president.'

Biden was certainly right that the honesty, or otherwise, of politicians was becoming a bigger issue for American voters in 1974 than ever before. Because that was the year when the drip-drip of revelations in the Watergate scandal that started in 1972 finally turned into the raging torrent that swept President Richard Nixon away. Nixon, the incumbent President, had won re-election in 1972 by a massive majority, beating his Democratic challenger in all states bar one. No previous American president at the time had ever had more votes cast for him than Nixon received that year.

In the context of crushing supremacy, it seems even more absurd that Nixon's re-election committee commissioned a break-in shortly before the election at

Washington's Watergate complex to tap the phones of prominent figures in the Democratic National Committee who were based there.

Nixon publicly reassured America, 'I can say categorically that . . . no one in the White House staff, no one in this administration, presently employed, was involved in this very bizarre incident.' Nixon himself was not behind the plot, remarking when he heard about the break-in, 'Who was the asshole that did that?'

It soon transpired, however, that the assholes in question were connected to Nixon's 'White House Plumbers', a team initially charged with preventing leaks of sensitive information, whose remit had expanded to include what was known as 'rat fucking', i.e. dirty tricks directed against political opponents. As the Watergate investigations reached deeper into the nefarious machinations of different parts of the White House, Nixon himself became involved in the attempted coverup, and that was what eventually brought him down.

Support for Nixon collapsed with the release of the 'smoking gun tapes' which revealed the president had been aware of the White House's connection to the break-ins soon after they happened, and had deliberately tried to cover it up. Faced with becoming the first president impeached in over 100 years and being forced from office, Nixon resigned in August 1974, less than two years after his electoral triumph.

One of the men who would have been certain to vote for the impeachment of the President, had the matter reached the Senate, was Joe Biden of Delaware, telling Kelley in the interview shortly before the release of the tapes, 'I would have voted for Mickey

Mouse against Richard Nixon. I despise that man.'
Biden was one of only three Democratic senators who
had earlier voted against Nixon's appointment of his
Defence Secretary, Elliot Richardson, as the new
attorney general in an attempt to save his presidency.

But he also made sure to argue for proper process
throughout Watergate, insisting, 'Let's not hang
[Nixon] before we have a trial . . . if we hang Watergate
around the Republicans and the people buy it, the
system goes under.' Throughout Biden's career, for
better or worse, defence of 'the system' would always
be near the forefront of his mind.

In just two years, Biden had gone from dealing
with garbage collection rezoning on New Castle
County Council to front-line involvement in the
greatest political scandal in the nation's history. But,
Watergate aside, Biden's first few years in the Senate
were relatively quiet. In keeping with his junior status,
he was allocated places on two relatively dull commit-
tees, the Public Works Committee and the Banking,
Housing, and Urban Affairs Committee. On the latter,
Biden did try and make some waves by introducing his
first bill which empowered the Federal Housing
Administration to hand over abandoned houses to
cities so that they could be regenerated. He also
suggested that the Senate should cut Nixon's budget
for the White House in half in response to the president having slashed spending on housing across the
nation.

Deteriorating neighbourhoods were increasingly
an issue in early 1970s as the growth which had begun
in the late 1940s finally ground to a halt. During the
long years of the post-war boom, the American
economy averaged nearly 4% annual growth. Unem-

ployment remained below 6% in all but two of the years in the period 1949-73.

Shortly after Nixon's election triumph, however, the surging American economy slumped. Runaway inflation, the oil crisis of 1973, and increasing competition from newly industrialised nations all played a part. By November 1973, the United States had fallen into a 'stagflation' (a recession that combines high inflation and high unemployment) that would last a year and a half and cause an estimated 2.3 million job losses (a post-war record)[2]. It was in this context that Biden could quip, 'considering what Nixon has done to the employment situation in this country, I'm damn grateful to be employed.'

By the time America emerged from recession, Nixon, the president of vice, had fallen, replaced by his Vice President, Gerald Ford (who controversially pardoned his predecessor to get him off the hook of facing criminal charges). Even with the recession officially over, America remained in a malaise of high inflation and nearly double-digit unemployment rates, which would not pass until the 1980s.

In this context, it was perhaps impolitic of Biden to flout the convention that new senators should be 'seen but not heard' and draw attention to himself by demanding a pay rise. 'We should flat out tell the American people we are worth our salt', he said during a debate on increasing senators' $42,000 annual salary. Although, he wanted to balance the pay rise by calling for senators to no longer be able to have any outside income.

His comments predictably attracted criticism in both Delaware and beyond. In New Hampshire, later to be the scene of his disastrous primary performance in 2020, the front page of the Manchester Union Leader declared, 'The voters of Delaware who elected this stupid, conceited jackass to the Senate should kick him in the rear to knock some sense into him, and then kick themselves [for] voting [for] such an idiot.'

Biden also attracted some rather positive publicity during his early years in the Senate. The Junior Chamber of Commerce celebrated him as one of 'America's Ten Outstanding Young Men', while the San Francisco Chronicle awarded him the prestigious accolade of being one of the ten best-dressed members of the Senate. In 1974, Time Magazine named him as one of their '200 Faces for the Future', and nearly every profile or article featured some suggestion that he would be a future presidential candidate.

'Let's do wait and see', he said when Kitty Kelley brought up the subject in his interview. Before adding, with reference to the age restriction of 35 for becoming president, 'Come back and talk to me in a few years. By then I'll be old enough to run. Right now, I'm too young. I'm probably the only senator you can really believe when he says he's not planning on running for president, at least not in 1976 . . .'

Through good publicity and bad, Biden was steadily becoming better known on the American political scene. But through it all, his boys remained his priority. Instead of relocating to Washington as he had planned before the accident, he remained at home in Wilmington, and every morning began with him waking the boys and taking them to school before commuting to work at the Senate on the Amtrak train. Every evening, he would run from the Senate to the station in Washington to get back home in time to tuck them in for bed.

An issue that surprisingly didn't come up in Biden's extensive interview with Kelley was the one that generated most controversy during his first term, caused him to fear for his re-election campaign, and which is still being debated during his current run for the presidency—desegregation busing.

7

'A LIBERAL TRAIN WRECK . . .'
THE DESEGREGATION BUSING
CONTROVERSY

The racial segregation of American schools has a history as old as the United States itself. It is a history that has been marked by day-to-day acts of discrimination and by the grand decisions of the highest court in the land, which has, on multiple occasions, reinforced the rights of states and schools to deny places to pupils on the basis of their skin colour.

In 1883, the Supreme Court ruled that part of the Civil Rights Act of 1875, which banned discrimination in public institutions such as schools, was unconstitutional. In 1896, the so-called 'Jim Crow' segregationist legislation of some (mainly southern) states was given further legal backing by the same court's verdict in the case of Plessy v. Ferguson, which permitted separate schools provided the quality of the facilities was equal[1]. Of course, in reality, a vast chasm separated the quality of the two types of school.

Throughout the 20th century, the issue of racially segregated schools continued to be hugely controversial and emotive. It appeared to have been settled in

1954 with the Supreme Court ruling in the case of Brown v. Board of Education, which declared that racial segregation in schools was unconstitutional. However, the court gave no guidance on how integration was to be achieved, leaving scope for further conflict over the following decades—conflict which reached a particular nadir in 1957, when the Governor of Arkansas deployed the National Guard to prevent 9 black children ('The Little Rock 9') from entering an all-white school.

In an attempt to meet the challenges of desegregation and the equalisation of educational opportunities, civil rights advocates across America supported the establishment of bus services to take black children to previously white-dominated schools (and vice versa). Busing became a particularly challenging issue for Joe Biden, a self-proclaimed civil rights activist representing a state that was fiercely opposed to the practice.

Biden's position on busing during the 1972 election was clear. He supported it in places like the southern states, where segregation had been imposed by law (de jure) but opposed it in places like his own state of Delaware, where segregation had occurred through socio-economic circumstances and patterns of settlement (de facto). It is easy to see how critics of Biden could portray this as him trying to 'have his cake and eat it', in the sense that he could still call himself a supporter of civil rights whilst playing to the concerns of the white majority of his constituents, who feared the enforced racial mixing of their schools.

In 1975, New Castle County Council was ordered to arrange for the integration of its schools, with busing to be the main means of moving black children from Wilmington out to the suburbs, and white suburban kids into the city. In his memoirs, Biden described busing as 'a liberal train wreck, [which] was tearing people apart'. He also made his feelings clear at the time, telling a local newspaper, 'I oppose busing, it's an asinine concept, the utility of which has never been proven to me.' Two anti-busing amendments which he introduced were initially approved by the Senate, although ultimately rejected later in the law-making process.

In the same year, he further justified his position with words which he may regret in the 2020 elections. 'I do not buy the concept, popular in the '60s, which said, "We have suppressed the black man for 300 years and the white man is now far ahead in the race for everything our society offers. In order to even the score, we must now give the black man a head start, or even hold the white man back, to even the race," I don't buy that. I don't feel responsible for the sins of my father and grandfather. I feel responsible for what the situation is today, for the sins of my own genera-tion. And I'll be damned if I feel responsible to pay for what happened 300 years ago.'

It was not the first time Biden had weighed in on matters related to race relations with words he would be unlikely to repeat in the 21st century. Back in 1970, he had told reporter Jane Harriman, 'I have some friends on the far left, and they can justify to me the murder of a white deaf mute for a nickel by five colored guys. They say the black men had been oppressed and so on. But they can't justify some Alabama farmers tar and feathering an old colored woman. I suspect the [American Civil Liberties Union] would leap to defend the five black guys. But no one would go down to help the "rednecks". They are both products of an environment. The truth is somewhere between the two poles. And rednecks are usually people with very real concerns, people who lack the education and skills to express themselves quietly and articulately.'

The concerns that Biden and many of his constituents had about desegregation busing saw him becoming allied politically, and in some cases, close friends, with those senators most strongly aligned with articulating the world view of the rednecks. Amongst them was Strom Thurmond of South Carolina, a man who once said, 'all the bayonets of the army cannot force the negro into our homes, into our schools, our churches and our places of recreation and amusement', and who accused Martin Luther King of 'demean[ing] his race and retard[ing] the advancement of his people.'

Biden's friendship with the likes of Thurmond is an (extreme) example of one of his selling points in his pitch to the American people in 2020, his ability to build bridges across traditional party lines at a time when political polarization is tearing the nation apart. Explaining, in 1986, how he could continue to be a supporter of civil rights but an opponent of busing, he described himself as an expert in moderation, saying, 'I've always viewed my role, what I've done best in the Senate, as one of the guys who kept the pendulum in the middle.'

Back in 1976, Biden had his first significant involvement in a presidential election, becoming the first senator to endorse Jimmy Carter, the former governor of Georgia, who eventually became the Democratic nominee to take on incumbent Gerald

Ford. Biden was rewarded with the chairmanship of Carter's National Campaign Steering Committee and even stood in for the candidate on several national speaking duties. However, shortly after Carter's triumph over Ford, the two men fell out. One of the causes was the vexed issue of desegregation busing, which led Biden to oppose, unsuccessfully, Carter's nomination of Wade McCree, a supporter of busing, for the post of solicitor general.

Biden had argued in 1975 that issues are less important in an election than a candidate's character because issues change so quickly. But by 1978, he was coming to fear that the school busing issue would undermine his own prospects of being returned to the Senate by the people of Delaware. On one of his daily commutes by train to Washington, Biden and his top aide, Ted Kaufman, worked out what their strategy of attack would be if they were the opposing Republican candidate in the elections scheduled for that year. It consisted of using Biden's history of support for civil rights to suggest that his opposition to busing was 'just a Trojan horse', and that, once elected, 'he'll pull the rug out from under the anti-busing lobby.'

Biden's fears show how big an issue busing was for his constituents. But in truth, he was associated strongly enough with the anti-busing campaign to have had no need to worry. In fact, as the Wilmington Morning News noted in 1978, 'the only substantive legislation bearing Biden's name to reach the nation's law books is the Biden-Eagleton Amendment, which has shut down efforts by the Department of Health, Education, and Welfare to achieve busing for school desegregation.' Biden's re-election in 1978 had none of the drama of his earlier struggle with Boggs. He easily overcame the Republican challenger, chicken farmer James H. Baxter, winning 58% of the votes to Baxter's 41%.

Biden's belief that issues change rapidly in American politics has also been directly contradicted by his experience with the issue of desegregation, which continues to be a live topic in the national debate, and a subject on which his former words and actions are often dug up and used against him.

A case in point: 44 years after busing was ordered in Wilmington, Biden found himself confronted on national television during the Democratic presidential candidate debates by one of the kindergartners whose education was at stake in the desegregation busing arguments of the '70s: a child who had grown up to be a senator herself, and one of his challengers for the Democratic nomination for the presidency, who some think may come to be his own choice for vice president—Kamala Harris.

Back in the late '70s, Biden was now a second-term senator with a gradually rising national profile and a coveted seat on the Foreign Relations Committee. He was also married for a second time, tying the knot in New York's UN chapel with Jill Jacobs, a fellow Pennsylvanian native who'd moved to Delaware in June 1977. Biden proposed at least five times before she finally accepted, showing a resilience even greater than he has in his three presidential bids, the first of which was launched in the following decade.[2]

8

'TO MY GENERATION HAS NOW COME THE CHALLENGE . . .' JOE BIDEN'S 1980S

The early 1980s were a bad time for the Democratic Party generally, but a good time for the career of Joe Biden. In the 1980 presidential election, Jimmy Carter was swept away by the landslide victory of former Hollywood actor Ronald Reagan. Carter was undermined by the ongoing underperformance of the American economy and his failed attempt to resolve the Iran Hostage Crisis, which had seen 52 Americans captured by supporters of Ayatollah Khomeini's Islamic Revolution in Tehran.

Biden was closely connected to the hostage crisis from his position on the Senate's Foreign Relations Committee. In April 1980, the Committee sent him on a mission to the Persian Gulf, during which he befriended a naval officer by the name of John McCain. Theirs was to become one of the most notable friendships across party lines in American political history, although one that was tested to its limits when they found themselves on the opposite sides of the ticket in the 2008 presidential elections.

Carter's fall in 1980 took with it twelve Democratic senators, neatly clearing space for Joe Biden's ascent to continue. In the reshuffle that followed, he became the most senior Democrat on the prestigious judiciary committee, chaired by his controversial friend Strom Thurmond. Biden's rise was not celebrated by civil rights activists concerned with his stance on busing, but he was quick to signal his willingness to do battle with Thurmond's plans to repeal elements of all of the most significant civil rights legislation of the 1960s.

Biden's ascent continued with an angry speech at the 1983 New Jersey Democratic Convention in Atlantic City. To the approval of the crowd, he attacked the current condition of his own party, accusing it of forgetting 'what got us this far and how we got here—moral indignation, decent instincts, a sense of shared sacrifice and mutual responsibility, and a set of national priorities that emphasized what we had in common . . . Instead of thinking of ourselves as Americans first, Democrats second, and members of interest groups third, we have begun to think in terms of special interests first and the greater interest second.'

At just 41, Biden was still a young voice within the party, and he concluded his speech with an emotive call to his generation to act in the common interest of America, invoking the spirits of the leaders of his youth—Martin Luther King and the Kennedy brothers[1]. 'To my generation has now come the challenge. In the days to come we will be tested on whether we have the moral courage, the realism, the idealism, the tenacity, and the ability to sacrifice some of the current comfort to invest in the future . . . I believe that this generation will rise to the challenge . . . The experts believe that, like the Democratic Party itself, the less than forty-year-old voters are prepared to sell their souls for some security, real or illusory. They have misjudged us. Just because our political heroes were murdered does not mean that the dream does not still live, buried deep in our broken hearts.'

From the stage, Biden could see tears in the eyes of his audience before they rose into a standing ovation. The nerve he struck that day did not go unnoticed in the national press, with positive feedback from the Washington Post contributing to a building momentum that suggested Biden would run for president in 1984.

However, it was not to be. Biden mulled it over but ruled himself out, citing his ongoing prioritisation of the needs of his sons—then young teenagers—over his political ambitions. 'If I were serious', he said, '[about a presidential bid] I'd have to devote two full years to running flat out . . . It's difficult to be the kind of father I want to be and go flat out for two years.'

Perhaps it was a wise political calculation, too— Biden knew he had little chance of winning the race to become the Democrats' chosen candidate, and perhaps preferred to keep his powder dry for 1988. Reagan was also in a very strong position as a popular president, having overseen a long-overdue upturn in the American economy, and he trounced the eventual Democratic candidate, Walter Mondale, in the '84 election. Reagan won in all states bar one and claimed 58.8% of the popular vote (a figure unequalled by any presidential candidate since).

Biden successfully defended his own senate seat

again in 1984, this time against a challenge from John Burris, who claims to have been put forward by a leader of the powerful du Pont family, Pete du Pont, who feared election defeat by Biden would harm his own presidential ambitions for 1988. Burris adopted a strategy that Biden himself would probably have approved of, trying to demonstrate weakness in his opponent's character. 'Our whole strategy', he recalled later, 'was to get Joe mad because he had such a short temper.' It worked in one debate during which Burris's questioning about Biden's attitude to the US's invasion of Grenada triggered a screamed response from the senator.

Similar outbursts have continued to plague Biden throughout his political career, but back in the 1984 senate election, they ultimately did nothing to undermine his campaign. Biden increased his majority, receiving over 60% of the votes cast. By now, he was the well-established figure able to trade, as his earlier opponent Boggs once had, on widespread recognition and positive perceptions across the state. As Burris summed it up, 'I was John Burris; he was Joe.'

Biden's generally moderate stance on many issues attracted criticism from some quarters, notably from leading civil rights activist, Rev. Jesse Jackson, who attacked the centrist Democratic Leadership Council (DLC) of which Biden was a member. Jackson accused them of 'combing their hair to the left like Kennedy, but moving their policies to the right like Reagan', adding that the DLC was made up of people who 'didn't march in the '60s and won't stand up in the '80s'. When asked by the press if his comments were a 'thinly veiled' attack on Biden, Jackson retorted that it was not even thinly veiled. His critique has continued up to the 2020 presidential race, with Jackson endorsing Biden's progressive rival, Bernie Sanders, for the Democratic nomination.

Biden was not going to let criticism get in the way of his rising national profile nor let it sway him in his attempts to link himself to the most prominent Irish American Democrat. At a speech in Iowa in late 1985, he invoked once again the ghost of Kennedy in an attempt to summon up the spirit of the early 1960s when the Democrats had successfully inspired the nation. 'It's time', he told the crowd, 'we heard the sound of the country singing and soaring in the dawn of a new day. It's time to restore America's soul. It's time to be on the march again. It's time to get America on the move again.' It was the sort of enthusiastic rhetoric that goes down well in the US, but the question remained—was it time for Joe Biden in '88?

He insisted it was not. Emphasising as always that his family, which by now included Ashley, his four-year-old daughter with Jill, came first. By early 1987, though, Biden observers would have noticed that he was increasingly spending his weekends in states like Iowa, New Hampshire, and South Carolina. What links those states? They are the first to vote in the primaries in which each party selects their candidate for president.

Meanwhile, he continued giving very well-received speeches around the country, so enthusing a crowd of Democrats in Sacramento, California that he realised, 'there was almost nothing to stop me making the run'. But that very same speech that convinced him to go for the presidency also contained hidden within in it a hint of the problems that would soon plunge him into controversy. Unnoticed at the time, a speechwriter had slipped into his address a handful of the words of Robert Kennedy, which Biden delivered to a cheering crowd without citing the source. An old ghost from Biden's past was about to return to haunt him.

But before old problems resurfaced, Biden suddenly found himself facing new challenges with his health. It began with headaches so severe that he was taking up to ten paracetamol per day to manage them. Biden was even forced to leave the stage during a speech in Nashua, New Hampshire, such was the pain he was feeling.

Apart from these ominous hints of trouble ahead, 1988 seemed to be shaping up to be Biden's year. The initial frontrunner for the Democratic nomination, Gary Hart, pulled out in May 1987, following a frenzy of media attention centred on allegations of womanising. The field was clearing for Biden to step in, and so he did with an announcement at Wilmington train station on 9 June 1987, that he was, after years of speculation, finally about to run for president.

Again evoking the spirit of his political hero, JFK, Biden told the assembled crowd and the watching nation, 'We must rekindle the fire of idealism in our society, for nothing suffocates the promise of America more than unbounded cynicism and indifference . . . I am absolutely convinced that this generation is poised to respond to this challenge . . . and this is the issue upon which I will stake my candidacy.'

The whole Biden family then took a specially-commissioned train bound, of course, for Washington. Biden was on his way to fulfilling his long-held ambition. What could possibly derail his plans?

9

'IN MY ZEAL TO REKINDLE IDEALISM, I HAVE MADE MISTAKES . . .' THE COLLAPSE OF BIDEN'S FIRST PRESIDENTIAL BID

Sometimes it is in moments of seeming triumph that the seeds of future disaster are sown. When the Democrats regained control of the Senate in the 1986 mid-term elections, Biden, the undistinguished law student, was elevated to chairmanship of the Judiciary Committee. It was exactly the sort of highly prestigious and influential appointment that he had long coveted, not least because it brought with it an important role in the decision-making process around the appointment of Supreme Court judges, with each presidential nomination having to go before the committee before proceeding to the Senate for confirmation.

However, as soon as Biden announced his candidacy for the 1988 election, he was faced with responding to Reagan's nomination of one of the most controversial judges in US history. His handling of the crisis threatened to overwhelm his presidential ambitions.

It is, of course, the characteristic of presidents to

seek to elevate those judges who share their own political convictions, and in some ways, their Supreme Court nominations can be the most lasting legacies of their presidency. Supreme Court judges, unlike presidents, are not restricted to a limited number of years of service, and their interpretations of the US Constitution determine the legal code of the land. If a president succeeds in stuffing the Supreme Court with judges from a particular political persuasion, he can create a legacy that lasts long beyond his own term.

Unsurprisingly, Reagan's Supreme Court nominee, Robert Bork, was an arch-conservative. He was also a deeply divisive figure, notorious both for his judgements, his pledge to overturn the civil rights judgements of the 1950s and 1960s, and for his role in the 'Saturday Night Massacre' at the height of the Watergate scandal. In October 1973, Nixon had shocked the nation by ordering his Attorney General, Elliot Richardson, to fire the special prosecutor leading the Watergate investigation. Richardson, however, refused and resigned. Nixon replaced him with a man willing to carry out the order, Robert Bork, who was apparently promised a seat on the Supreme Court in return for his loyalty.

Nixon's presidency did not survive long enough for him to fulfil his promise, but in July 1987, Reagan did it for him, creating a storm of criticism from liberals all over the land. Bork became only the second Supreme Court nomination opposed by the American Civil Liberties Union, and he was also attacked by feminist and civil rights organisations[1]. In the Senate, Ted Kennedy (JFK's sole surviving brother) threw fuel on the fire with his claims that 'Robert Bork's America is a land in which women would be forced into back-alley abortions, blacks would sit at segregated lunch counters, rogue police could break down citizens' doors in midnight raids, school children could not be taught about evolution, writers and artists could be censored at the whim of the Government, and the doors of the Federal courts would be shut on the fingers of millions of citizens for whom the judiciary is—and is often the only—protector of the individual rights that are the heart of our democracy.'

As chair of the committee charged with confirming Bork's appointment, Biden found himself under enormous scrutiny. Like Jason and his Argonauts, he was confronted with the prospect of being crushed between clashing rocks. On one side, there was liberal disapproval of Bork, which demanded that Biden vocally oppose the appointment, and on the other was conservatives' professed adherence to correct protocol and procedure, which clamped down on any criticism he did make as a failing in his duty of impartiality.

In a difficult situation, Biden did not help himself with an initial reaction, which suggested to conservative supporters of Bork that their man would not receive a fair hearing. 'I will resist', he said shortly after the nomination was announced, 'any attempt by this administration to do indirectly what it has failed to do in the Congress—and that is impose an ideological agenda upon our jurisprudence.' After making further private comments against Bork, Biden was criticised in the press with the Washington Post, saying, 'While claiming that Judge Bork will have a full and fair hearing, Senator Joseph Biden this week has pledged to civil right groups that he will lead the opposition to the confirmation. As the Queen of Hearts said to Alice, "Sentence first—verdict afterwards."'

Despite his early mistakes and criticism from both sides of the debate, Biden eventually won praise for his handling of the controversial appointment. Patrick Leahy, a Democratic senator also on the committee, told him, 'I have heard from an awful lot of people both for and against Judge Bork who have complimented you on the fact that you have even handedly arranged to have witnesses on both sides, and have handled them even handedly.' Republican Strom Thurmond, a friend of Biden's but a supporter of Bork, also praised the chairman for his handling of the committee. Terence Moran, a reporter for Legal Times, wrote that Biden had 'acquitted himself superbly' in what was 'the greatest constitutional debate in recent years.'

Biden won more than praise; he was also successful in overseeing a rejection of Bork both by the Judiciary Committee and the full Senate. Reagan reneged on his threat to return with an equally controversial nomination, and proposed moderate conservative, Anthony Kennedy, who was unanimously approved by the Senate. Commenting on the significance of the Bork decision, Mark Gitenstein, one of Biden's advisers on the Committee, said it was 'the only time we won a big jurisdictional fight over the direction of the Supreme Court . . . we defeated Bork and got two moderate justices . . . we got a whole generation of decent jurisprudence because of that fight.'

It was a fight that Biden had won at great cost to his presidential ambitions. So focused was he on the furore surrounding the Bork case that he left himself with little time to prepare for such duties as debates with his fellow Democratic candidates, with disastrous consequences.

Biden, at this time, had been greatly inspired by a speech given by the leader of the UK Labour Party, Neil Kinnock, in May 1987. In it, Kinnock had posed the question, 'Why am I the first Kinnock in a thousand generations to be able to get to university? Why is Glenys [his wife] the first woman in her family in a thousand generations to be able to get to university? Was it because all our predecessors were "thick"? Did they lack talent—those people who could sing, and play, and recite and write poetry . . . Was it because they were weak? Those people who could work eight hours underground and then come up and play football? . . . Of course not. It was because there was no platform upon which they could stand.'

Biden was so inspired, especially by the final line, that he was at this time regularly giving a version of the speech himself, linking it to his own status as the first Biden to go into higher education. Normally when Biden gave the speech, he gave full credit to Kinnock for his words. However, on one occasion during a debate with his fellow candidates in Iowa in August 1987, Biden, unprepared and with his mind still on the Bork case, delivered the speech without citation.

'Why', he asked his audience, 'is it that Joe Biden is the first in his family ever to go to a university? Why is it that my wife who is sitting out there in the audience is the first in her family to ever go to college? Is it because our fathers and mothers were not bright? Is it because I'm the first Biden in a thousand generations to get a college and a graduate degree that I was smarter than the rest?'

He went on to echo other parts of the speech, including the sections referencing a family history of coal mining and the lack of a platform to stand upon, which Biden later described as 'my argument at its heart.' The lack of reference to Kinnock in the speech came back to bite Biden severely, after an aide to the campaign of his rival, Michael Dukakis, the eventual winner of the Democratic nomination, alerted the press[2].

Unfortunately for Biden, when the story broke, it was followed shortly afterwards by evidence of further plagiarism. Examining his previous record with new zeal, the press discovered unattributed borrowings from Robert Kennedy in the speech Biden had recently given in Sacramento, which had convinced him of the feasibility of running for president. Looking back further in his record, the old case of the missing citations which had got him into trouble at law school resurfaced. A picture was starting to form of a man who spoke the grand rhetoric of idealism but who seemed, in reality, as slippery as the stereotypical used car salesman.

The story quickly gathered such momentum that it threatened to sweep away Biden's campaign altogether. In the new scrutiny of all of Biden's previous words, further inconsistencies, half-truths, and outright lies were revealed. A conversation with a heckler was reported in which Biden claimed to have graduated in the top half of his law school class (he'd actually finished 76th out of 85). Biden's previous claims to have been a marcher in the civil rights movement were also dug up and found to be, at best, an overstated version of the truth that he had been involved in a single diner walkout and one protest against a segregated cinema.

In the face of the mounting wave of criticism, Biden concluded that he was faced with a choice between either trying to rescue his campaign or continuing to deal with his obligations on the Judiciary Committee. He announced his decision at a press conference, given during a lunch break in the Bork proceedings. 'Although it's awfully clear to me what choice I have to make,' he told the assembled press, 'I have to tell you honestly I do it with incredible reluctance—it makes me angry. I'm angry with myself . . . for having put myself in the position of having to make this choice . . . But, folks, be that as it may, I have concluded that I will stop being a candidate for President of the United States.'

'Quite frankly in my zeal to rekindle idealism, I have made mistakes . . . now the exaggerated shadow of those mistakes has begun to obscure the essence of my candidacy, the essence of Joe Biden . . . There will be other presidential campaigns and I'll be there, out front', he predicted, accurately, 'but there may not be other opportunities for me to influence President Reagan's choice for the Supreme Court.'

Returning to the Committee with his presidential dreams in tatters and his precious honour besmirched, Biden was comforted by the words of an opponent, Republican Senator Alan Simpson, who told him the Senate 'can be savage and barbaric and yet also caring and supportive. I think we politicians move at such a pace in our lives, we really do not have time to savour victory or anguish defeat. And that is good. But I [have a] hunch that care and support will surface now, and it always has, and so heal up quickly. We need you here in the fray so we can box each other around. I would not want to miss any of that.'

The 1980s had begun with high hopes for Biden, but as the decade drew towards its conclusion, it was about to get even worse as the senator faced a new problem that threatened to take him out of the fray for good.

10

'HAD HE STAYED IN THE RACE HE'D BE DEAD ALREADY . . .' FROM THE LAST RITES TO THE WORLD STAGE

On 10 February 1988, a call was made from the Saint Francis Hospital in Wilmington to summon a Catholic priest to come and read the last rites for Senator Joseph Biden. That morning, he'd been found collapsed on the floor of his hotel room in Iowa by his friend Bob Cunningham. His friend helped him home by plane to Wilmington, where he was admitted to hospital immediately. A spinal tap revealed blood in his spinal fluid, and the doctors realised he'd suffered an aneurysm, bleeding at the base of his brain. Life-saving surgery was the only option, with no guarantee that it would succeed.

Taken to a second hospital for surgery, the doctors explained to Jill and a conscious Joe Biden that if he survived, one of the side effects could be loss of the ability to speak. Biden, never one to miss an opportunity to make a wise crack, replied, 'I wish that had happened last summer.' One of the surgeons who performed the operation would make a joke of his own in 2019, backing Biden's latest presidential bid with the words, 'He's the only politician in Washington I'm sure has a brain, because I've seen it.'

The procedure was a success, although the doctors identified the need for further surgery on a second aneurysm they'd identified during the process, and later, on a blood clot on his lung. Overall, Biden spent seven months away from the Senate recuperating. The whole episode taught Jill Biden that sometimes moments of seeming misfortune contain within them the seeds of future salvation. 'All I remember thinking to myself', she later told the Washington Post, 'was, "My God, had he stayed in the [presidential] race, he'd be dead already."'

Biden was back in electoral action in 1990, successfully defended his Senate seat for a third time, and once again increased his majority despite his recent downfall on the national stage. Reaffirmed by voters in his home state, Biden soon found himself playing a familiar—and unwanted—major role on the national stage, again chairing a Senate Judiciary Committee hearing into a controversial Supreme Court nomination. But this time, the controversy would explode even more spectacularly than it had in the case of Bork, leaving further questions about Biden's ability to handle a crisis.

The nominee in this case was Clarence Thomas, an African American with conservative credentials, selected by President Bush as a replacement for the retiring civil rights icon, Thurgood Marshall. As with Bork, Thomas's nomination was opposed by civil rights and feminist organisations, the latter focusing on his position on women's rights to an abortion. Towards the end of the hearings, Biden was also made aware of allegations of sexual harassment against

Thomas by Anita Hill, a law professor who had previously worked with him at the Equal Employment Opportunities Commission.

In her later testimony, Hill detailed her allegations, saying, '[Thomas] spoke about acts that he had seen in pornographic films involving such matters as women having sex with animals and films showing group sex or rape scenes . . . On several occasions, Thomas told me graphically of his own sexual prowess . . . and made embarrassing references to a porn star by the name of Long Dong Silver.'

Were the allegations to have been made in the modern context of the #MeToo movement, it seems likely that Biden would have acted differently. However, back in 1991, he hesitated, unsure of how to act, and ultimately only passed on the details of the allegations to Democratic committee members at the last moment, not wanting to make them public while Hill wished to remain anonymous[1]. The hearings were not delayed to allow further investigations into her claims. Biden ultimately voted against recommending Thomas to the Senate, but remarkably, in light of his knowledge of the accusations, he made it clear his opposition was purely based on Thomas's views, adding, 'for this senator, there is no question with respect to the nominee's character.'

Ultimately, with a 7-7 tie in voting, the committee came to the Senate with no clear recommendation concerning Thomas's appointment. Before the full Senate could vote on the confirmation, the story of Hill's allegations broke in the press. Two further women came forward, substantiating Hill's story with accusations of their own against Thomas. Biden was forced to defend his conduct, with awkward questions asked about why the vote was being passed to a Senate unaware of the allegations against Thomas. He defended himself by insisting that he was respecting Hill's own wishes to not go public with her story.

Nevertheless, in light of the accusations becoming public knowledge, the committee's televised hearings were reopened with Professor Hill called as a witness to detail the sexual harassment she claimed to have suffered at the hands of Thomas. An angry and defiant Thomas blamed racism and derided the process as 'a high tech lynching for uppity blacks who in any way deign to think for themselves.' Hill, herself African American, later wrote that she found Thomas's accusations ironic given that he had long belittled anybody who blamed racism for their struggles.

Testimony was read to the committee from the other women who had accused Thomas, but they were not called to testify in the face of opposition from the Republicans (and some Democrats) on the committee. Biden has since claimed that it was the women's own choice not to testify. Others have argued that, had they have faced the committee, the result would have been Thomas's nomination being rejected, but as it was in a vote of the full Senate, he was confirmed by 52 votes to 48 (despite Biden voting against him). As of 2020, Clarence Thomas is the longest-serving current member of the Supreme Court and has frequently been identified as the most conservative member of that body. The potential for further clashes with his old adversary still exists if Biden wins his latest presidential bid in 2020.

The Clarence Thomas case was not Biden's only controversial action in the '90s still being debated a quarter of a century later during his latest Presidential bid. In 1994, a bill which he authored, the 'Violent Crime Control and Law Enforcement Act', was passed by Congress, becoming the largest crime bill in US history. The bill was written in a context of rising concern about violent crime across the nation and concern within the Democratic Party that they were seen as being weak on crime relative to their Republican rivals (by this point, the Democrats were back in the White House under President Bill Clinton[2]).

Biden was, in many ways, the ideal person to draft a bill intended to show the Democrats flexing their muscles on crime, having given ample previous evidence of his willingness to defy the party's liberal wing. The bill created 60 new death penalties, 70 enhanced penalties, 100,000 new police officers and allocated an extra nearly $10 billion in funding for prisons, helping them to establish 125,000 new cells. The passing of the Act also helped Biden himself to refute the perennial charge that he was all words but no action.

Liberal critics of the Act have argued that it led to mass incarceration across America, particularly of black people, although statistics show that prison populations were already rapidly increasing before 1994, and that the rate of increase actually slowed shortly after the Act was passed. Further, most prisoners are held in state prisons, which were largely unaffected by the federal legislation, not least because most states claimed to have already gone 'tough on crime' before they received extra directions from Congress. Biden's own claims that the Act 'restored American cities' are also not really backed up by research evidence, which suggests that legislation has had little impact on the falling violent crime rates seen across the nation since the 1990s[3].

Biden has sought to distance himself from some aspects of the legislation, particularly the notorious 'three strikes and you're out' provisions, which he called 'wacko' even in 1994. At the same time, he's been happy to refer to the bill in its entirety as 'the Biden Crime Bill' and to emphasise how proud he is of elements of it, such as the 10-year Federal Assault Weapons Ban and the Violence Against Women Act. The latter Act, which came with $1.6 billion of extra funding, so appealed to liberal senators that even such a celebrated progressive as Bernie Sanders voted in favour of the crime bill because of how strongly he supported that aspect of it[4].

The final year of the 1990s saw Biden vote in favour of the Financial Services Modernization Act, unsurprisingly given that he represents Delaware, the corporation-friendly state that is home to a large number of America's banks. The Act repealed the Glass-Steagall law, dating from the Great Depression of the 1930s, which had prevented banks from owning insurance businesses and securities.

In the wake of the Act, the number of banks in America shrunk drastically, with the sector becoming increasingly condensed in a smaller number of huge firms. This, combined with the repeal of Glass-Stea-gall, created the conditions which led to the financial crisis that began in America in 2007 and went global in 2008. With the benefit of hindsight in 2014, Biden said, 'The only vote I can think of that I've ever cast in my years in the Senate that I regret—and I did it out of loyalty, and I wasn't aware that it was gonna be as bad as it was—was Glass-Steagall.'

Away from the home front, the 1990s saw Biden, the second highest-ranking Democrat on the Senate's Foreign Relations Committee, playing an increasingly greater role on a rapidly changing international stage. The fall of the Berlin Wall in 1989 was the most dramatic moment of the collapse of Communism in Eastern Europe, followed very shortly afterwards by the dissolution of the Soviet Union itself (on 26th December 1991) and the end of the Cold War.

As America became the sole superpower, political scientist Francis Fukuyama made his famous declaration that the world was witnessing, 'the end of history', meaning that liberal democracy had triumphed and would become and remain the only form of government in the world. In the same year of 1992, Samuel Huntington began to popularise the opposing thesis of 'the clash of civilisations', predicting ongoing conflict based on what he saw as the fundamental differences between western culture and that of much of the rest of the world.

Evidence that Huntington's supporters could draw upon to support his theory included the conflict that would come to be known as the First Iraq War, which built up in 1990 and exploded in early 1991. Biden made clear his opposition to President Bush's plans for military intervention to force Saddam Hussein's Iraqi forces out of occupied Kuwait, advocating the use of economic sanctions instead. 'The United States', he declared, 'should not be the principal policeman of the world.'

He also stuck to the principle that the president should not be able to send the nation to war without Congressional approval, arguing, 'Americans once lived under a system where one man had unfettered choice to decide by himself whether we could go to war or not go to war, and we launched a revolution to free ourselves from the tyranny of such a system.'

Despite Biden's evocation of a protracted struggle comparable to Vietnam, and Saddam Hussein's threats of 'the mother of all battles', the war was actually resolved swiftly and successfully. The Iraqis were beaten out of Kuwait by Operation Desert Storm, and Bush Sr refrained from pushing far into Iraq itself, leaving the mantle of 'liberator' to be picked up by his son 15 years later. Biden's attacks on the war would be used in the future as ammunition against him by hawkish Republicans as evidence that the Democrats could not be trusted to respond sufficiently to the challenges that America would increasingly face from terrorism and 'rogue states'.

Biden did back military intervention in the former Yugoslavia, after the collapse of communism saw the country split into warring states, with Serbia's Slobodan Milosevic intending to wipe out the Croat and Muslim populations of Bosnia and Herzegovina. Biden claims that on a visit to the Serbian capital of Belgrade, he confronted Milosevic and accused him of being 'a damn war criminal'. He certainly did, from within the Senate, call for arms to be sent to the Bosnians and for air strikes against the Serbs, and was highly critical of the general lack of action. 'We have stood by', he said, 'we the world—and watched in the twilight moments of the twentieth century something that no-one thought would ever happen again in Europe.'

Biden eventually got what he was pushing for, with NATO Air Strikes in Bosnia and, subsequently, in Kosovo, helping to end Serbian expansionism and the massacres euphemistically termed 'ethnic cleansing'[5]. Milosevic was eventually arrested in 2001 and put on trial as a war criminal in 2002. But by that time, the world had changed altogether from the twilight of the 20th century into a new millennium that was marked so near the moment of its birth with a shock to the United States like none ever before.

11

'I WOULD NOT BE ANYBODY'S
VICE PRESIDENT, PERIOD . . .'
FROM 9/11 TO BIDEN'S SECOND
PRESIDENTIAL BID

On the 10th September 2001, Joe Biden was addressing
the National Press Club in Washington, attacking
plans being formulated by the new President, George
W. Bush, to resurrect Reagan's old plans for a so-called
'Star Wars' defence system against an international
nuclear missile strike[1]. Biden said presciently that such
an expensive system would 'address the least likely
threat, while the real threat comes to this country in
the hold of a ship, the belly of a plane, or smuggled
into a city in the middle of the night in a vial in a
backpack.'

The next morning, Biden was on his way back to
Washington on the train from Wilmington, as usual,
when news started to spread in the carriage about a
plane having crashed into one of the twin towers of
the World Trade Centre in New York. Biden's wife Jill
called him while she was watching the scenes on the
news, then suddenly, she interrupted their conversation, exclaiming, 'Oh my God . . . another plane . . . the
other tower!'

Biden arrived in Washington to find 'a brown haze of smoke hanging in the otherwise crystal clear sky beyond the Capitol Dome', its source the Pentagon headquarters of the US Department of Defence, which had been struck by a third hijacked plane. Literally out of the blue, two of the United States' most iconic locations had been transformed into war zones, and there was a sense then all around the watching world that anything was possible.

What actually happened next was the start of an extremely protracted American military engagement in Afghanistan and the Second Iraq War. By now, Biden was the Chairman of the Foreign Affairs Committee, and recognised as one of the most knowledgeable of senators on international affairs[2]. In such capacity, Biden was closely involved in the build-up and execution of both conflicts.

The justification for the invasion of Afghanistan was simple; the extremist Islamic State was home to Osama bin Laden, the leader of the Al-Qaeda terrorist organisation responsible for 9/11. Bin Laden was allied with Afghanistan's Taliban government, who had come to power following decades of struggle in the country, encompassing a lengthy conflict against the Soviet Union (during which bin Laden was a US ally) and various civil wars.

Biden supported the US strikes on Afghanistan which began just weeks after 9/11. It initially appeared that these attacks had achieved many of their objectives, with the Taliban rapidly overthrown and a democracy established under the leadership of Hamid Karzai[3]. On a mission to Afghanistan, Biden found a country still in fear (accurately, as it turned out) of the Taliban's return, and desperate for funding to improve the country. Such funds were diverted, however, before the Afghan mission was truly complete, in favour of pursuing the next target of the neo-conservative hawks guiding President Bush—Iraq.

By the time of Bush's infamous 'axis of evil' speech, much attention was being drawn by the administration to the 'weapons of mass destruction' that Saddam Hussein was allegedly developing and stockpiling with the intention of using them against America and its allies. Critics argued that this was merely a smokescreen for Bush's plans to bring about regime change in Iraq, while at the same time, securing access to the country's abundant oil supplies.

In the run-up to what began to appear as an inevitable conflict in Iraq, Biden was asking the right questions about what the plans would be for after Hussein was removed. 'It would be a tragedy', he argued presciently, 'if we removed a tyrant and left chaos in its wake.' He also co-sponsored a Senate resolution that would have authorised the use of force only in the event of all other options having been exhausted.

However, under pressure from the leaders of the Democrats in the House of Representatives and the Senate, Biden eventually relented and voted on 11th October 2002 for Bush's resolution to use force in Iraq. The cynical argument of the leading Democrats had been that their party might fare better in the forthcoming mid-term elections if the electorate were not casting their votes in the shadow of an ongoing debate about whether to go to war or not. Biden later claimed he believed that showing America was united behind Bush would make it more likely that Hussein would be compelled to comply with the UN's demands to disarm.

Biden insisted in his comments during the debate that war must still be only a last resort. But it was too late; with congressional approval granted, the die was cast, and he would be left with a long time to rue a decision that he would come to see as a mistake. Although the Iraqi army was rapidly defeated after the invasion in March 2003, the much-discussed weapons of mass destruction were never found, and the situation in Iraq rapidly descended into a bloody anarchy which neither the interim government nor the United States and its allies could control.

Despite the disastrous state of Iraq, President Bush won re-election in 2004, defeating Biden's friend, Senator John Kerry, by 37 electoral college votes. Biden's disenchantment with the Bush administration was sufficient to help him overcome any reticence about running for President again following the fiasco of his campaign in 1988.

So determined was he to bring about a change in the direction of American politics that he made a very early declaration of his own candidacy, telling CBS News in June 2005, 'It is my intention to seek the nomination.' He confirmed the same in January 2007, and around the same time, cast a disparaging look at one of his fellow potential candidates. 'I'd be a little surprised if he actually does run', he said of Senator Barack Obama of Illinois.

This time around, Biden was not using the soaring but insubstantial rhetoric of generational change which had characterised his previous presidential bid. Instead, he was stressing his experience on both the international and domestic stages. However, on the very day he filed the official paperwork for his application to be the presidential candidate, Biden's old habit of saying whatever was on his mind without the application of any filter soon landed him in trouble again.

The problem stemmed from further remarks about Obama, who he described as 'the first mainstream African American, who is articulate and bright and clean and a nice-looking guy.'[4] Reflecting back on those words, Biden's campaign adviser, Larry Rasky, said, 'The day the campaign ended was the day it started.'

The Biden campaign did, however, keep running, despite being hamstrung by his own words and problems attracting the funding that is essential for any presidential bid[5]. He tried to gain traction with his legitimate claim to have the most international experience out of any of the candidates seeking to wake America up from the nightmare of Iraq. He proposed repealing the 2002 authorisation for the use of force in the country and managing a 'much narrower and achievable mission for our troops', leading to full withdrawal by early 2008.

But none of this made any great impact with voters. In the Iowa caucuses, Biden attracted only 1% of votes, finishing a distant fifth. His second presidential campaign was over, although this time, he felt much happier than after his previous challenge, pleased that he had fought a substantial campaign in contrast to his 1988 effort.

Nevertheless, even before the end of his campaign, Biden had been very clear about one thing: 'I absolutely can say with certainty I would not be anybody's vice-president, period. End of story. I guarantee I will not do it.' That pledge, however, was about to be tested in a most unexpected way.

12

'CHANGE HAS COME TO AMERICA . . .' THE OBAMA-BIDEN 2008 CAMPAIGN

In stark contrast to Joe Biden, Barack Hussein Obama was still a first-term senator when he launched his bid for the presidency in 2007. Born in Hawaii to a Kenyan father and a mother from Kansas, he first burst onto the American political scene with his land-slide victory in the 2004 US Senate primary election in Illinois, which was followed by a keynote address at that year's Democratic National Convention. Obama electrified the party with a speech that focused on 'the audacity of hope' and raised in many the truly auda-cious hope that the self-proclaimed 'skinny kid with a funny name' could become the first African American president.

As early as January 2008, Obama was courting Biden, asking for his endorsement in the forthcoming struggle with Hillary Clinton for the Democratic nomination. Biden played a straight bat, saying he would not endorse any candidates, but pledged his full support to whichever candidate was finally selected in the battle to defeat the Republicans' chosen successor to George W. Bush, whose second and final term was coming to a close.

In the run-up to the eventual presidential election, it became increasingly clear that whoever won would face enormous challenges from the financial crisis which had begun in America in 2007, and which went global in 2008. One of the key causes of the crisis was the bursting of the subprime mortgage bubble, which brought about the collapse of banking institutions deemed too big to fail. In the face of overwhelming economic crisis, Obama's upbeat message, 'Yes We Can', struck a chord with Americans yearning for change.

Whilst campaigning, Obama identified the repeal of the depression-era Glass-Steagall laws, which Biden had voted for, as a stepping stone to the financial crisis. This, however, did not stop him from speaking to Biden about a potential role in his campaign and administration. 'If you win,' Biden told him, 'I'll do anything you ask me to.' Obama cautioned him in response, saying, 'Be careful, because I may ask you a lot.' In June 2008, Obama did eventually win the Democratic nomination, overturning the odds in a hard-fought battle against the establishment candidate, Hillary Clinton.

Faced with a presidential campaign against the Republican nominee, John McCain, Obama had to make a crucial choice about who would be his running mate and vice president in the event of electoral success. The Obama team drew up an extensive longlist, featuring such luminaries as the recently defeated Hillary Clinton. However, in the end, he settled on Biden as his first choice.

Was it because Biden brought decades of high-level

domestic and foreign policy experience, including
confronting dictators and being stranded in
Afghanistan, helping to fill in a significant gap in
Obama's own CV? Or was it because, despite everything that had happened in his long and eventful
career, Joe Biden was ultimately still 'the kid from
Scranton', able to appeal to blue-collar America in the
crucial swing states of the Rust Belt in a way that,
arguably, the Harvard educated intellectual Obama
could not?

'We knew Biden could be somewhat long-winded
and had a history of colouring outside the lines a bit',
said Obama's advisor David Plouffe euphemistically
when looking back at the appointment. 'But honestly
that was very appealing to Obama, because he wanted
someone to give him the unvarnished truth. What do
you need in a vice president? He knows and understands Congress, had great foreign policy and
domestic experience. He had the whole package from
a [vice presidential] standpoint.'

Perhaps Obama even suspected that a tendency
towards making blunders when speaking was
regarded by sections of the American public as a sign
of a down-to-earth authenticity—what other lesson
could be drawn from the two electoral successes of the
notoriously gaffe-prone George W. Bush[1]?

More seriously, Biden had demonstrated over his
long career an ability to command respect and build
bridges across Party divides in Congress, something
that would prove invaluable to Obama in office. He'd
also impressed Obama with his performances during
the presidential candidates' debates[2].

Finally, and crucially, Obama and his team were
confident that Biden would strike voters as being a

man with sufficient experience and clout to step up to the top job in the event that something happened to the president[3].

Obama summed up the qualities that had persuaded him to put his faith in Biden when introducing his running mate to a crowd of supporters in Springfield, Illinois. Linking his choice to the key message of his campaign, he said Biden had 'brought change to Washington, but Washington hasn't changed him. He's an expert on foreign policy whose heart and values are firmly rooted in the middle class. He has stared down dictators and spoken out for America's cops and firefighters. He is uniquely suited to be my partner as we work to put our country back on track.'

The Vice-Presidential nomination brought a new nationwide prominence to Biden's career. His first headline appearance at the Democratic National Convention gave him ample time to enjoy his new status with a half-hour speech, which was, in typical Biden fashion, very much a family affair. He was introduced by his son Beau, who was now the Attorney General of Delaware and also a member of the National Guard about to be deployed to Iraq.

Biden then gave what Time magazine described as 'an unhurried discourse about his family and middle-class struggles with a conversational emotion that few American politicians can match . . . The homage to his [91-year-old] mother sitting in the gallery was one of the emotional high points of the convention so far— her great American face beamed as he talked with obvious love about her.'

Biden told the audience about his mother's old-fashioned approach to conflict resolution. 'When I got knocked down by guys bigger than me she sent me back out and demanded that I bloody their nose so I could walk down the street the next day.' It is not known if Mrs Biden (who was, by then, 91 years old), would have been in favour of her son bloodying the noses of several members of the American press corps; but it is certain that the media used Biden's elevation to the top ranks of the Democratic Party as a new opportunity to try to knock him down—both through the recycling of some old scandals, and the uncovering of some new ones.

In a foreshadowing of scandals to come, several of the new stories revolved around Biden's second son, Hunter—a lawyer, lobbyist and serial founder of companies. One story focused on Hunter and Biden's brother, Jimmy, being sued by an ex-business partner. Further revelations concerned Hunter receiving consultancy fees from Delaware-based credit card giant, MBNA, at a time when Biden was supporting a bankruptcy protection bill for which the credit card industry had lobbied.

Biden's campaigning for Obama's presidential bid began with a return, alongside his mother, to the house he was born in on North Washington Avenue in Scranton, for a picnic with the current owners. The event chimed with the image the Obama campaign was keen to sell of Biden, an 'ordinary Joe', who had risen from humble beginnings, understood the concerns of the average American, and had dedicated his life to fighting for them. But at the same time, some of the press wanted to dig behind the image and uncover Biden's ties to the world of corporate America, which so dominates the state he had long represented—Delaware.

Particular attention was paid to Biden's own relationship with MBNA, including the sale of his house to an MBNA executive and the generous campaign contributions Biden had received from employees of that company[4]. Biden's voting record on matters related to the banking industry, so powerful in Delaware, showed that he had supported its deregulation and also backed efforts that made it harder for Americans to get out of debt to student loan and credit card companies[5].

But none of these stories made any significant impact on the Obama-Biden campaign. Nor did the majority of Biden's predictable verbal gaffes. The 2008 vintage included saying Hillary Clinton was 'more qualified than I am to be vice president', arguing that 'when the stock market crashed Roosevelt got on the television' (even though he was not president at that time, and television barely existed), and most embarrassingly, exhorting a wheelchair-bound state senator to get to his feet at a rally with the words, 'Stand up, Chuck, let 'em see you!'

Biden's only significant error was one of his off-message meanderings when he told the crowd at a fund-raising event in October, 'Mark my words. It will not be six months till the world tests Barack Obama like they did John Kennedy. Watch, we're going to have an international crisis, a generated crisis to test the mettle of this guy.' Biden had apparently talked himself into an immediate crisis with his prospective boss, with a furious Obama apparently asking his advisers, 'How many times is Biden going to say something stupid?' Biden made fewer appearances in the last weeks of the campaign to make sure he did not make any more damaging mistakes.

Republican nominee John McCain, a decorated

Vietnam veteran, latched on to Biden's words in Seattle as evidence of Obama's dangerous inexperience. It made no difference. As soon as polls closed on the evening of the 4th November, US television networks called the election for Obama, and as the results came in, it was clear that they were right. The Obama-Biden ticket won 53% of the popular vote and 365 of the 538 electoral college votes.

That night, in front of a jubilant crowd of nearly a quarter of a million in Chicago's Grant Park, America's first African American president addressed the nation. Evoking the spirit of Martin Luther King, he declared, 'Change has come to America . . . The road ahead will be long, our climb will be steep. We may not get there in one year, or even in one term, but America, I have never been more hopeful than I am tonight that we will get there.' When after his speech he returned to the stage, it was with his family and the man who would be by his side as he discovered just how hard the road would be—Joe Biden.

Inevitably amidst the jubilation surrounding Obama's historic victory was the fact that Biden had also successfully defended his Senate seat yet again. His victory in Delaware made him the youngest man, at age 66, to be elected to the Senate seven times. Mere days after being sworn in, there for the final time, he was obliged to stand down in order to go and receive the oath of office of the Vice President of the United States. As of 20th January 2009, Joe Biden, the stuttering son of a used car salesman from Scranton, was just a heartbeat away from the top job in the world.

13

'THE SKUNK AT THE FAMILY PICNIC . . .' BIDEN'S FIRST TERM AS VICE PRESIDENT

Biden's notorious prediction that Obama would be tested by a new international crisis within 60 days of coming to power did not come true. But the new president inherited such a wide range of problems from the Bush administration, both at home and abroad, that his ability to handle a crisis was actually tested from day one. To help deal with the many challenges the Obama administration faced, Biden was soon given the hands-on vice-presidential role that he had insisted upon when discussing taking the job.

That said, the extent of Biden's role as vice president was notably and deliberately curtailed relative to his immediate predecessor, Dick Cheney, who was seen by many as the power behind the throne during the Bush administration, pulling the strings of a puppet president. Obama made it clear from the outset that he would be the decision-maker, but Biden was to be by his side throughout as a more experienced adviser. The president compared his deputy in the early months of the administration to a basketball player 'who does a bunch of things that don't show up in the stat sheet.'

Taking advantage of Biden's foreign policy expertise, Obama soon deployed him on a mission to Pakistan, Afghanistan, and Iraq, charging him with coming up with recommendations for how the administration should proceed in that troubled region. Biden made the case a renewed focus on defeating Al-Qaeda and its leadership in the region.

America's apparent rapid success in Afghanistan had quickly proved illusory, with the Taliban and Al-Qaeda merely melting away into the mountains and returning frequently to strike at allied forces and the Afghan government. By this time, nearly seven years of US efforts had failed to capture the elusive Osama bin Laden. Biden's recommendation regarding Al-Qaeda was echoed by subsequent official reports. However, Biden did oppose Obama's eventual strategy of deploying 21,000 extra troops in Afghanistan, a policy pushed by new Secretary of State, Hillary Clinton.

The renewed focus on destroying Al-Qaeda bore fruit within Obama's first term, as unconfirmed reports came back to the White House that Osama bin Laden had finally been tracked down. Not to some cave on the wild Afghan-Pakistani border, as had long been assumed, but to a mansion in Abbottabad, a tourist centre only 120 km from the capital of Pakistan, just over a kilometre from a Pakistani military academy.

Biden's exact role in the run-up to the raid, however, continues to be a source of controversy. In its aftermath, he stated that he had told the president he should 'not go' for it until he had confirmation that bin Laden was inside the compound—a version of events that was also repeated in several other accounts written by people who were around the table in that crucial meeting. However, Biden has subsequently added to that story by saying that when he left the meeting and was alone with the president, he advised him, 'Mr President, follow your instincts. Mine are that you should do it, but follow your instincts.'

Of course, only Obama could confirm what happened in a private conversation between himself and Biden. What is certain is that the day after the meeting, Obama returned to the White House and gave his order with a single word: 'Go.' Biden was by the president's side in the situation room as his top national security team followed the mission by drone, as US Navy Seals burst into bin Laden's compound and killed him. Within 24 hours, his body was being buried in the Arabian Sea, in a bag filled with iron chains to make sure it would never float to the surface. It was the 2nd of May 2011, a few months short of the tenth anniversary of 9/11.

The legacy of 9/11 and Bush's response to it continued to cast a long shadow over the Obama presidency, and Biden also became heavily involved in the administration's attempts to reconstruct Iraq. Apparently, Obama handed Biden this responsibility during a national security meeting in the first year of his presidency with the words, 'Joe, you do Iraq', in the manner, according to the New Yorker, of someone 'doling out household chores.' Biden took his responsibilities seriously, with frequent visits and calls to Iraq, but the horrific mess there ultimately proved beyond his ability to clean up.

Biden's position on Iraq during his candidacy for

the 2008 elections had been to advocate the creation of a relatively loose federation of three states, one for each of the warring factions in the country (Sunni, Shi'a and Kurds). Inside the administration, however, he was forced to toe the line that Iraq would not be so divided, and decided to throw his support behind Prime Minister Nuri al-Maliki, whom he believed would both hold the country together[1].

US policy in Iraq was guided by Obama's pledge to pull troops out, which was initially achieved in December 2011. The country they left behind, however, was far from the liberated, liberal democracy envisioned by the most optimistic proponents of the war that had begun 8 years earlier. Iraq remained, despite the billions of dollars spent on its reconstruction, a shattered nation still racked by inter-ethnic conflict, which would only worsen in the absence of the US army, compelling further intervention by Obama in his second term.

On the home front, one of Obama's first successes was convincing Congress to inject an estimated $787 billion dollars into the US economy through the American Recovery and Reinvestment Act, a stimulus package intended to counteract the impact of the devastating financial crash of 2008[2]. Obama allocated Biden an oversight role, monitoring spending and the implementation of the Recovery Act across the country.

The stimulus package was passed with virtually no support from the Republicans, with every single Republican in the House of Representatives voting against it, and only three in the Senate voting in its favour. Those Republican Senators who did back it had been courted by Biden, using his well-honed ability to build bridges across party lines.

The other huge piece of domestic legislation from the early years of the Obama administration was the Patient Protection and Affordable Care Act, colloquially referred to as 'Obamacare', which extended health coverage to millions of previously uninsured Americans and sought to lower costs for middle-income families through subsidies. On the day Obama signed the Act into law, a microphone picked up an enthused Biden telling the President that it was 'a big fucking deal', broadcasting his words out to the nation, live.

Obama's first two years in power saw him living the dream scenario for any president, as his party had the majority of both the House of Representatives and the Senate, giving him the freedom to pursue his legislative priorities without much concern about what the Republican minority thought about it.

The mid-term elections of November 2010, however, saw a monumental shift, with the Republicans gaining 63 seats and a majority in the House of Representatives, giving the rival party enormous power to restrain Obama's agenda of change. Obama was punished by voters critical of his healthcare reforms and of the unemployment rate, which remained over 9% despite his efforts at stimulus. The Democrats would not regain control of the House during Obama's presidency.

In this new context, Biden's skill at negotiating and building consensus across party lines became increasingly invaluable to the Obama administration. Biden helped win Senate ratification in December 2010 for the 'New START (Strategic Arms Reduction Treaty)' which

Obama had negotiated with Russia, committing both countries to reducing their stockpiles of nuclear missile launchers. In the same month on the domestic front, he helped negotiate with the Republicans a compromise tax package, which included temporarily extending some of the tax cuts introduced by President Bush.

Perhaps Biden's most dramatic moment of cross-party negotiation came in 2011, when a dispute between the President and Congress was threatening to push the United States government into defaulting on its debts, plummeting the world into a new economic crisis. With two days to go before default and talks on the bill required to resolve it stalled, the Obama administration made what one leading aide called, 'our last play'—calling on Joe Biden.

Despite already being seen by many as something of a figure of fun, Biden had something that none of Obama's bright, younger staff could bring, a 25-year working relationship with Mitch McConnell, the Republican leader of the Senate. A senior member of the Republican Party staff confirmed the importance of the vice president's role to the deal, saying, 'Biden's the only guy with real negotiating authority, and [McConnell] knows that his word is good. He was a key to the deal.' A report on Politico said it showed that 'even the most dysfunctional political system can be made functional through the injection of fear, finesse and Joe Biden's old friendships.'

Despite mid-term electoral defeats, the Obama-Biden ticket comfortably won re-election in 2012 against the Republican challengers, Mitt Romney and Paul Ryan[3]. Although, there was a time in which Biden's appearance on that ticket was in doubt; secret meetings involving top Obama aides discussed the possibility of replacing him with Hillary Clinton in an attempt to redress the President's falling popularity. However, when the results of polls showed the change having minimal impact on Obama's election prospects, his campaign decided to stick with Biden.

Inevitably, there were a few occasions on the campaign trail when they might have regretted their decision. Most notably when Biden blurted out his support for same-sex marriage, pre-empting by several months a long-planned Obama statement on the same issue. Obama was on the record as saying that his position on same-sex marriage was evolving. Biden effectively forced the president to declare that the evolution had become a revolution, with Obama stating days later that he wanted to 'affirm that same-sex couples should be able to get married.'

Overall, there seems to have been plenty of times during the first term when a degree of tension existed between the slick and smooth Obama and Biden's rather more rough edges. But Obama also came to appreciate Biden's qualities as well. Not least of which was his willingness to 'be the skunk at the family picnic', as one Obama adviser put it. The adviser referred to a contrarian quality that was described rather more flatteringly by Obama himself when he said, 'The best thing about Joe is that when we get everybody together, he really forces people to think and defend their positions, to look at things from every angle, and that is very valuable for me.'

14

'THE BEST VICE PRESIDENT AMERICA'S EVER HAD . . .' TRIUMPH AND TRAGEDY IN BIDEN'S SECOND TERM

Obama's second term did not begin with the same wave of optimism that had greeted his first. Despite some early legislative landmarks post-2008, his message of hope and change had run into a brick wall of political reality, and his loss of the House in 2010 would severely hamstring his attempts to remodel America in the ways his supporters had once dreamed. During his second term, the situation worsened with the loss of the Senate in 2014. Sadly, 'Yes We Can' was to become increasingly 'No We Can't' as Obama endured a full second term as a 'lame duck' President.

Throughout Obama's second term, there was increasing speculation that Biden would follow in the footsteps of many previous vice presidents by putting himself forward as a candidate for the presidency when the 2016 elections came around. However, further tragedy in the Biden family was eventually to overshadow the end of his service as vice president, and to rule him out of contention in 2016.

The legislative struggles Obama was to endure

were illustrated early in his second term, with his attempts to pass new gun control measures in response to the Sandy Hook Elementary School shooting in Newtown, Connecticut in December 2012. Gun control had been an issue that Obama had not previously confronted, possibly due to concern about losing votes in key swing states, but the country's deadliest school shooting compelled him to act.

Biden, who had a successful record on gun control with his assault rifle ban in 1994, was heavily involved in the proposed new legislation. But even his experience could not help the proposals to pass the Republican-dominated Senate, on what Obama called 'A shameful day for Washington.'

In general, Biden was not called upon to deal with Congress quite so much in Obama's second term, despite previous successes. Some leading figures in the Democratic party, most notably Senate majority leader Harry Reid, decided against involving him in negotiations over issues such as the federal government shutdown and the debt ceiling crisis of 2013. Reid's reasoning was that Biden had given too much away in his previous negotiations with McConnell when breaking similar impasses during Obama's first term.

Biden was appointed in 2014 as co-chair of the new White House Task Force to Protect Students from Sexual Assault, responding to studies that showed, in the words of a White House Press Release, that '1 in 5 women is a survivor of attempted or completed sexual violence whilst at college.' Again, Biden's work here built upon the successes of the 1994 crime bill with which he was so heavily involved, specifically the Violence Against Women Act. In a speech at the University of New Hampshire, Biden directly addressed the men in the audience, saying, 'Look guys . . . no matter what a girl does, no matter how she's dressed, no matter how much she's had to drink —it's never, never, never, never, never okay to touch her without her consent.'

Embarrassingly for Biden, allegations that he has repeatedly touched women and girls inappropriately have surfaced in the years since that speech. In January 2015, Democratic Senator Chris Coons of Delaware had to defend Biden after footage showed his 13-year-old daughter looking uncomfortable as the vice president took her arm and whispered to her at her father's swearing-in ceremony. Coons told Fox News, 'No, she doesn't think the vice president is creepy. He's known my kids their whole lives. Joe was just being thoughtful . . . He was leaning forward and whispering some encouragement to her . . . He was being Joe.'

'America shouldn't tolerate "Biden being Biden",' argued an article in Time Magazine later that same year, which focused on footage of him rubbing the shoulders of Stephanie Carter at the swearing-in ceremony for her husband, Defense Secretary Ashton Carter. Maintaining a theme from previous criticism, the article referred to Biden as 'Creepy Uncle Joe'. Biden's defenders stressed that he is a tactile politician who reaches out to people, literally, to offer support. Further allegations against Biden of similarly inappropriate conduct and touching without consent were to surface in the years to come in the wake of the international #MeToo movement.

Away from the domestic front, Biden continued to play a significant role on the international stage during Obama's second term. The worsening situation in the Middle East continued to occupy his attention.

The Syrian Civil War, which had begun during Obama's first term, continued to worsen and saw the rise of a new force in the region, the self-proclaimed Islamic State of Iraq and Syria (ISIS) which exploited the instability of both countries to carve out territory for itself and to impose its extremist interpretation of Islam.

Biden supported the President's decision to arm rebels to fight against the forces of Syria's President Assad and ISIS, and threatened ISIS that 'We will follow them to the gates of hell until they are brought to justice' in response to the beheading of American journalists they had taken prisoner.

Meanwhile, the descent of Iraq into further violence in 2014, as ISIS spread throughout the country and unleashed genocide against the Kurdish Yazidis, suggested to some a need to reappraise Biden's previously-ridiculed plan to divide the country into three semi-autonomous ethnic states. 'Was Biden right?' an article in Politico asked, quoting Biden's own New York Times piece from 2007 which had argued, 'some will say moving toward strong regionalism would ignite sectarian cleansing. But that's exactly what is going on already, in ever-bigger waves . . . Others will argue that it would lead to partition. But a breakup is already underway. As it was in Bosnia, a strong federal system is a viable means to prevent both perils in Iraq.'

Meanwhile, back in Delaware, speculation was mounting concerning the apparent retreat from public life of Biden's son, Beau, the state's former attorney general who had been rumoured to be planning a bid for the governorship. An article by local journalist, Jonathan Starkey, in January 2015, questioned why a man recently considered a 'rising star' had 'made very few public appearances and has not delivered public remarks in months.' A Republican Delaware Senator, Greg Lavelle, was even quoted in the article calling Beau Biden's absence 'disrespectful' to voters. The terrible truth soon emerged.

On 30th May 2015, Beau Biden died of brain cancer at the Walter Reed National Military Medical Centre in Maryland. His family had kept secret the extent of his illness as he had battled it in the final years of his life, so it came as a great shock to many when news of his death broke. The son who Joe Biden nearly lost when he was just a little child had finally been taken from him at the age of just 46. 'It's unfathomable,' said David Axelrod, Obama's one-time political chief, 'to a lot of us who know Biden—and I think most Americans feel they do by now—to see how much sadness could visit one man and one family.'

Biden's book, 'Promise Me Dad: A Year of Hope, Hardship and Purpose', gave his personal account of his struggle with the death of his oldest son. The book's title comes from a conversation Biden had with his son before the worst of his illness was apparent. 'Promise me, Dad, that no matter what happens, you're going to be all right. Give me your word, Dad, that you're going to be all right. Promise me, Dad.' 'I'm going to be okay, Beau.' 'No, Dad . . . Give me your word as a Biden . . . Promise me, Dad.' 'I promised,' Biden wrote.

Biden's great love for his son shined throughout the book. 'Beau Biden, at age 45, was Joe Biden 2.0,' the proud father wrote. 'He had all the best of me, but with the bugs and flaws engineered out.' Biden was confident that Beau himself would run for president one day.

Throughout Biden's second term as vice president, there had been mounting speculation that he would run for the top job himself at the end of Obama's eight years. The speculation continued even after Beau's death, fuelled by a story that his deathbed wish had been for his father to pursue the presidency. Biden scotched the specific detail of that rumour in his book, but did confirm that it had indeed been Beau's wish in the final months of his life that his father would proceed with a campaign for the presidency.

Honouring Beau's wishes, and buoyed by a belief that he could finally win, Biden continued to make preparations for his third presidential challenge, even going so far as to draft his announcement speech in October 2015. But ultimately, he was forced to concede that his heart was still too broken to bear facing a presidential campaign.

As he puts it in his book, the moment of realisation finally came when a mention of Beau caused him to break down in public. 'I felt a lump rise in my throat,' Biden wrote. 'My breathing suddenly became shallower and my voice cracked. I was afraid I would be overwhelmed by emotion, and I think the audience could see it. I waved and hustled over to the car. This was no way for a presidential candidate to act in public.'

Biden concluded that the time was not right for him to run, because 'grief is a process that respects no schedule and no timetable.' Biden has the unwanted gift of understanding grief more than most, having gone through the unimaginable pain of burying his own child, not once, but twice—the first a baby, the second a man with children of his own. Recognising this, some have called him 'America's mourner in chief'. He has certainly shown a great willingness to take on that role and a genuine aptitude for comforting others going through the same pain that he has faced.

Biden recounts driving just weeks after Beau's death to a Methodist church in Charleston, where nine African American parishioners had been murdered by a white supremacist. He went because 'the act of consoling had always made me feel a little better and I was hungry to feel better.' He talks of often giving mourners his private number and inviting them to call him if ever they needed someone to talk to, and he quotes the reassurance that he often gives to mourners, 'I know from experience . . . that the time will come, the time will come when [your loved one's] memory will bring a smile to your lips before it brings a tear to your eyes. That's when you know—it's going to be OK. I know it's hard to believe it will happen, but I promise you, I promise you it will happen.'

In 2015, Biden had not yet reached that place, and was not ready to run for the presidency in 2016. He did, however, still have vice-presidential duties to complete, right up until the January 2017 date for handover to the new administration. With just over a week remaining before the formal end of his tenure, Biden was surprised by President Obama awarding him the Presidential Medal of Freedom, with distinction, America's highest civilian honour. Obama described Biden as 'A lion of American history' and 'the best vice president America's ever had.'

15

'WE ARE IN A BATTLE FOR THE SOUL OF THIS NATION . . .' THE RUN-UP TO THE 2020 ELECTION

The eventual winner of the Democratic nomination for the presidency in 2016 was Hillary Clinton, who had the backing of President Obama and saw off a strong and determined challenge from the veteran socialist, Senator Bernie Sanders. Clinton, however, was subsequently defeated by the Republicans' shock candidate, controversial billionaire and reality TV star, Donald Trump.

With Trump threatening to repeal much of the Obama legacy, it is unsurprising that Biden has been a staunch critic of the new president. In 2017, he told Trump to 'grow up' and 'stop tweeting', referring to the president's habit of making proclamations via the social media platform. Biden himself took to Twitter to warn of climate change's 'existential threat to our future' while attacking Trump's pledge to pull out of the Obama era Paris Climate Accord.

He did, however, argue against impeaching President Trump in 2018, saying, 'I don't think there's a basis for doing that right now.' Ironically, when the basis finally did come, it revolved, unwittingly, around Biden himself and his son, Hunter.

Before that storm blew up, Biden faced further criticism concerning inappropriate physical contact. In March 2019, Lucy Flores, a former Nevada state assemblywoman, alleged that Biden had, without her consent, touched her shoulders, smelt her hair, and kissed the back of her neck. Biden claimed not to remember any of the alleged behaviour.

A further five women came forward with allegations of inappropriate physical contact. Biden offered what critics called a 'non-apology', saying, 'Social norms are changing. I understand that, and I've heard what these women are saying. Politics to me has always been about making connections, but I will be more mindful of personal space in the future. That's my responsibility and I will meet it.'

In April 2019, Biden ended months of speculation with a video on Twitter in which he announced, 'We are in the battle for the soul of this nation. If we give Donald Trump eight years in the White House, he will forever and fundamentally alter the character of this nation. And I cannot stand by and watch that happen . . . The core values of this nation, our standing in the world, our very democracy—everything that has made America America—is at stake. That's why today I'm announcing my candidacy for President of the United States.'

Trump tweeted, somewhat less idealistically, in response, 'Welcome to the race Sleepy Joe. I only hope you have the intelligence, long in doubt, to wage a successful primary campaign.' Trump has already given clear indications that part of his strategy in the election will be to make claims that Biden's mental faculties are fading with age, rendering him unfit for the presidency. At age 77, on election night, Biden could become the oldest man elected to a first term as president, breaking a record set by Trump himself, who, at 74 by election night, is not much younger than Biden. Their combined age of 151 at the time of the election would set a new record for the oldest pair of participants in a presidential race.

Some of Biden's statements during the election campaign thus far may appear to lend credence to Trump's insults about the waning of his mental faculties. Calling a student who asked him a question in New Hampshire a 'lying, dog-faced pony soldier' raised some eyebrows amongst onlookers. On another occasion, he managed to get his own name, and that of the president he served under, wrong, when he encouraged 'folks who want to nominate a Democrat, a lifelong Democrat, a proud Democrat, an OBiden-Bama Democrat, join us.' Seasoned observers of Biden will be well aware, however, that his history of such gaffes extends well before the current presidential campaign.

The extent to which Trump feels genuinely threatened by the man he has so disparaged can perhaps be gauged by the events that led to the President's impeachment. In September 2019, reports began to break that Trump had pressed Volodymyr Zelensky, a comedian turned president of Ukraine, to look into alleged misdemeanours concerning Joe Biden and his son, Hunter. The allegations related to Burisma Holdings, an energy company that employed Hunter Biden.

According to the accusations, Joe Biden had abused his power in government by withholding $1 billion worth of aid to the Ukrainian government in order to force them to fire a prosecutor who was investigating Burisma. In fact, Biden was enacting official administration policy when pressing for the firing of the prosecutor, who was dismissed partly because of the lack of progress in his investigations of Burisma. There is no evidence that either Biden did anything wrong.

Ironically, Trump himself withheld military aid to Ukraine to pressure Zelensky to publicly declare he was investigating the Bidens. Following revelations from an anonymous whistle-blower, the House of Representatives launched an impeachment enquiry into Trump, which led to the publication of a 300-page report which concluded that 'President Trump, personally and acting through agents . . . solicited the interference of a foreign government, Ukraine, to benefit his re-election. In furtherance of this scheme, President Trump conditioned official acts on a public announcement by the new Ukrainian President, Volodymyr Zelensky, of politically-motivated investigations, including one into Joe Biden, one of Trump's domestic political opponents.'

The impeachment trial of Trump ended, unsurprisingly, with his acquittal by the Republican-controlled Senate. Trump has continued to maintain unsubstantiated attacks against the Bidens over the Ukraine issue, arguing in one of his campaign advertisements that 'when President Trump asks Ukraine to investigate corruption, the Democrats want to impeach him and their media lapdogs fall in line.'

With the impeachment scandal adding extra fuel to

the fire, if Biden does become the Democrats' presidential nomination, as seems most likely, his battle with Trump threatens to be one of the most bitterly contested and nastiest elections in American presidential history.

16

'THE MEASURE OF A MAN . . .'

Twenty-four hours is a long time in politics, according to the cliché, in which context a month can seem like several lifetimes. In the time that's elapsed since the introduction to this book was written, all the conventions of American life and politics have come under threat from the novel coronavirus pandemic which has swept the globe, shutting down countries and entire continents.

Although Biden still seems overwhelmingly the favourite to win the Democratic primaries, the future of that process, and possibly even the election itself, is in doubt. At the time of writing, America is largely on lockdown and Biden's campaign is virtually paused. A politician who loves to get close to the crowds is self-isolating in his basement, broadcasting messages which are largely unheard. Such is the focus on the president and his response to an unprecedented crisis in American life. Such has been Biden's disappearance from the scene that the hashtag #wheresjoe has been trending on Twitter.

One thing that can be said with a degree of confidence is that the American people's view of the way in which Trump has handled this issue seems likely to be the deciding factor in this election. If he is deemed to have acquitted himself well against this threat, then the initial boost the crisis has brought to his approval ratings will surely be sustained into November (assuming the election does take place then). If the American people's judgement is that Trump has failed the nation in a way that could be catastrophic, then surely they will be unforgiving at the ballot box.

In some ways, Biden, locked away in his basement, is a prisoner of fate, rendered powerless in a way that no presidential challenger has ever been before. But if Biden's history teaches us anything, it's that what appears to be fate can be overcome, that circumstances which appear certain to destroy can be transcended, and, perhaps most of all, that getting into predictions about politics is always a risky business. So, let us, in this especially uncertain time, conclude with that which can be said with certainty.

As with any politician with such a long and prominent career, Joe Biden divides opinion. To his detractors on the left, he's a pseudo-liberal who talked up his civil rights credentials whilst voting down desegregation busing and befriending segregationists, a Democrat with Republican tendencies, and a corporate stooge, who put himself on the wrong side at the crucial moment in modern American history, voting with George W. Bush to unleash anarchy upon Iraq. To his detractors on the right, he's a lying career politician, the personification of the forces in Washington that Donald Trump claimed he would fight with his infamous slogan, 'drain the swamp.' Critics on both the right and the left would unite in seeing him as a windbag and a plagiarist, with an embarrassing track record of talking himself into trouble.

To his champions, Biden epitomises the decent and honest politician, a brave man who has not allowed tragedy to get in the way of his commitment to service, and who has not allowed his commitment to service to get in the way of his commitment to his family. His life story and career seems to hark back to various American 'golden ages', depending on what you view as golden. His life spans a carefree '50s childhood, through the liberal dreaming of the '60s, through a less-partisan time of cross-party collaboration, to most recently being at the heart of the Obama era, when the government was led by a man who appeared to many to fulfil the dream of an American statesman, a man who chose Biden as his second in command and lionised him as 'America's greatest ever vice president'.

But, surely, both Biden's detractors and champions would have to agree that one characteristic he has undoubtedly epitomised over his 50-year career is durability. In that context, let us imagine for a moment that his father's dictum is indeed true. That the measure of a man truly is how he responds to being knocked down. If that really is the case, then Joe Biden Jr, still standing after all he's been through, and standing for president no less, has got some claim as the greatest American politician of them all—irrespective of what happens in November 2020 and beyond.

JOE BIDEN'S 2020 POLICIES

As of April 2020, Joe Biden has given lots of indications about the policy positions that he would take in the presidential election. His policies include building on the legacy of the Obama administration with some more progressive proposals, responding to the rise of Bernie Sanders and his supporters' increasing influence on the Democratic Party. What we currently know about the policies of a potential President Biden is detailed below.

The Economy

Biden proposes increasing the federal minimum wage to $15 per hour (from the current $7.25) and then allowing it to go up in line with inflation. These proposals, which were shared by most of the Democratic candidates for 2020, go further than Hillary Clinton did with her proposals in 2016 to raise the minimum wage to $12 per hour. Biden's campaign also supports allowing workers to take paid leave in the event of having to care for a sick family member or a newborn child.

The Biden campaign has also given some relatively muted support to the concept of making reparations for slavery. Kate Bedingfield, his Communications Director, has been quoted as saying America should 'gather the data necessary to have an informed conversation about reparations.' Biden has so far stopped short of endorsing bills proposed in both the House and the Senate to form a commission to make concrete proposals about reparations.

Taxation

Biden proposes to increase taxes for corporations and the wealthy. He wants to raise the corporate income tax rate to 28% (from 21%) and to introduce a 15% minimum tax on corporations with at least $100 million in net profits. He also wishes to see a modest increase in the top income tax rate (for individuals earning over $510,000)—from 37% to 39.6%—and would increase the capital gains tax rate for people with income of over $1 million.

Immigration

Immigration has been one of the most divisive issues in America in recent years, with Trump's infamous (and still unfulfilled) pledge to build a wall across the Mexican border the centrepiece of his 2016 campaign. As of the end of 2019, only 93 miles of the wall had been constructed.

Biden remains in favour of maintaining criminal penalties for illegal immigration. Although he has also, in common with the vast majority of Democratic candidates, advocated for finding ways to extend US citizenship to the so-called 'Dreamers' (a term derived from the DREAM Act, which proposed a path for these people to become permanent residents of the

United States, but which has been repeatedly rejected by Congress).

Health Care

Biden favours incremental health care reforms to build on the Affordable Care Act ('Obamacare') of 2010, with the possibility of adding a public option in the future (although stopping way short of a 'Medicare for All' national health service). Prior to full implementation of Obamacare in 2014, 44 million Americans were without health insurance. That figure then decreased year on year until 2018, when the number of uninsured Americans rose again. Biden's health care proposals will focus on trying to extend coverage to the 27.5 million Americans who are still uninsured.

Americans spend an estimated $460 billion on pharmaceutical drugs each year, a figure which is pushed up by the very expensive prices of such medicine in the US. On average, people in other developed countries spend 56% less than consumers in the US when buying the same drugs. Biden proposes to reduce this discrepancy by establishing an independent board to compare prices and set them accordingly.

Education

As the husband of a schoolteacher, Biden has been keen to stress his understanding of the world of education and its needs. In which context, it is unsurprising that he supports pay rises for teachers, although his proposals in this area do not go as far as those that have been advocated by others candidates such as Bernie Sanders. In other areas of education policy Biden is sticking with policies from the Obama era which went unimplemented. For example, offering two years of community college or technical school for free.

Some of his policy positions represent a change in stance from the party line under Obama. For example, charter schools, 'semi-autonomous public schools that receive public funds'[1], were promoted under the previous administration. Biden now supports some curbs on charter schools, opposing those that operate for-profit, saying they '[siphon] off money for our public schools, which are already in enough trouble.'

On the contentious issue of student debt, Biden has a track record of being on the side of the loan companies. While Sanders demands the cancelling of all student debt, Biden has, typically, been much less radical with calls to fix and simplify the Public Service Loan Forgiveness Program, an existing and so far largely ineffective scheme to cancel the debts of those who work in public service for at least ten years.

Criminal Justice

On criminal justice it is perhaps surprising to find Biden, previously proud of trying to eliminate the Democrats' reputation for being soft on crime, sharing many of the same policy positions as progressive Bernie Sanders. For example, Biden supports abolishing the death penalty, terminating the federal government's practice of contracting private companies to run prisons, and ending cash bail, which has been criticised for favouring more affluent people over those with low incomes.

In order to reduce the extent of incarceration across America, Biden proposes providing funding to states who prioritise prevention over imprisonment, and also agrees with Sanders about reforming mandatory minimum sentences. He has even advocated reforming some aspects of the criminal justice system brought in by his own 1994 Crime Act, most notably calling for an end to the cocaine sentencing disparity. Since 1994, courts have sentenced people convicted on charges related to crack cocaine much more harshly than those using other types of cocaine, which has had a disproportionate impact on African Americans.

On marijuana, Biden proposes to maintain the policy of letting individual states make their own decisions about whether or not to legalise, although he has also made comments which suggest he might support full legalisation, subject to medical advice. He also agrees with removing previous convictions for marijuana-related offences from people's records.

Gun Control

'Guns, guns, guns', said Biden from the floor of the Senate in 1994, 'the single most contentious issue in the 22 years that I have been here that relates to criminal justice'.

Now, 26 years later, the issue is, if anything, even more contentious. US civilians own a total of 393 million guns, nearly 50% of the total of civilian-owned guns in the entire world. However, the epidemic of school shootings have eroded, although far from destroyed, support for the still highly influential National Rifle Association (NRA). A Gallup poll in 2019 found that for only the second time in 30 years, more US citizens (49%) had a negative view of the NRA than a positive one (48%).

A confrontation on the campaign trail illustrated the divisiveness of the issue, with a worker in Detroit accusing Biden of trying to 'diminish our second amendment right [to bear weapons] and take away our guns'. To which Biden, a gun owner himself, replied, 'you're full of shit.'

Back in 1994, Biden successfully introduced a ten-year ban on assault weapons as part of his Crime Bill. Now, in 2020, he is proposing further bans on the sale of assault weapons, a (voluntary) national buy-back programme for such guns, and the establishment of a national firearm registry. Biden is also in favour of universal background checks for people seeking to buy guns.

Environment and Agriculture

Unlike Trump, Biden is clear about the danger of climate change, and has committed to fighting it. His proposal to expand the use of nuclear power is opposed by many in the environmental movement, but does have significant support from some scientists who stress its potential for reducing carbon emissions relative to fossil fuels.

As part of the same commitment to reducing emissions, Biden also advocates a carbon tax and is in favour of not allowing any new exploitation of oil and gas reserves on federal lands. Fossil fuels taken from federal lands accounted for one quarter of the US's total emissions in the decade up to 2014. He has also discussed radically expanding a current voluntary programme to pay farmers to adopt climate friendly practices, with the aim of reaching net-zero emissions from agriculture.

In the field of agriculture, Biden proposes to increase protection for small and medium-sized farming enterprises against the giant agribusinesses that dominate the market. His proposals, however, are based on increasing the effectiveness of existing laws, rather than bringing in radical new challenges to the agribusiness industry. He has also proposed expanding protections for farm workers.

Transport

Biden plans for a $1.3 trillion investment in transport infrastructure with the intention of reducing economic inequality (by improving access to transport in poor areas), creating jobs, and helping to combat climate change. His ambitious plans would be funded by increased taxation of the very wealthy and reductions in subsidies paid to the fossil fuel industry.

Military

The US spends far more on its military than any other country in the world. Its annual expenditure of over $600 billion represents around one-third of the entire world's military spending. Biden, who has a mixed record on supporting the US's various recent wars, is in favour of further increasing military spending. He also remains in favour of keeping US troops deployed in Afghanistan and Iraq.

Trade

Biden has been critical of Trump's use of tariffs as a means of waging trade wars on other countries, most notably China, arguing that they do damage to the American economy. Although Biden did take a more combative stance towards China himself in recent debates, criticising issues such as breaking World Trade Organisation rules and stealing American intellectual property.

Biden has given qualified approval to the USMCA (United States Mexico Canada Agreement) on free trade, and supports joining the CPTPP (Comprehensive and Progressive Agreement for Trans-Pacific Partnership), arguing, 'either China's going to write the rules of the road for the 21st century on trade, or we are.'

Technology

Biden's election could be bad news for online social media giants. He is in favour of removing sections of a law which protects these from legal action relating to posts that their users have made on their platforms. He is also in favour of investigations to see whether any of these companies have broken antitrust laws designed to prevent monopolies.

Campaign Finance

Biden favours overturning the Supreme Court's 2010 decision which allows unlimited spending on election campaigns, seeing this as an essential step to fixing America's 'broken politics.' Biden has previously said, 'the United States constitution says "we the people", not "we the donors"'.

Biden believes his policy proposals taken together will achieve his vision of an America of 'equal opportunity, equal rights and equal justice.' 'It's time', his campaign tells the American people, 'to dig deep and remember that our best days still lie ahead.' Whether that is true for Joe Biden himself and his 2020 presidential campaign remains to be seen.

NOTES

'A POLITICAL MIRACLE UNLIKE ANYTHING IN MODERN PRESIDENTIAL POLITICS . . .'

1. For the sake of simplicity, the process by which each party selects its candidate for the presidential election is referred to throughout this book as 'the primaries'. Although the process actually encompasses both primaries (which are run by state governments) and caucuses (which are run by state political parties) with exact arrangements varying from state to state.
2. In a typical Biden moment, he managed to get the two of them mixed up, at one point taking his wife's hand and declaring that she was his little sister.

1. 'THE MEASURE OF A MAN . . .' JOE BIDEN'S BIRTH AND ROOTS

1. Joe Biden's father also carried the Robinette middle name. Although slightly unusual sounding, it's nothing compared to the middle name of Donald Trump's father—Frederick Christ Trump.
2. The term 'Rust Belt' refers to the portion of north-eastern America that suffered from deindustrialisation and economic decline in the late 20th century.
3. So great is Biden's association with his home state that he used to be referred to as Pennsylvania's third senator.

2. 'HE'S GOING TO BE PRESIDENT OF THE UNITED STATES!' BIDEN'S POLITICAL AWAKENING IN THE '50S AND '60S

1. The tone of some of the debate during that election can be gauged from the title of a popular talk given by a pastor in Okla-

homa on the subject of the candidate in question, 'Al Smith and the Forces of Hell.'

2. The popular vote (i.e. the % voting for each candidate across the whole nation) does not actually determine the outcome of a US presidential election. Instead, there is an electoral college system in which each state has a certain number of electoral college votes (depending on its population). Whichever candidate wins a majority in each state gets all of its electoral college votes, and whichever candidate takes an overall majority of electoral college votes wins the presidency.

3. 'A COAT AND TIE GUY WHO WOULD DO EVERYTHING CORRECTLY . . .' BIDEN'S PATH INTO POLITICS

1. According to an article in Mother Jones, there are 'nearly twice as many Delaware-incorporated companies as there are Delaware voters.' The tiny state's strategy for success has long been focused on creating as hospitable an environment as possible for businesses, encouraging many companies operating elsewhere to register themselves in Delaware.

4. 'I WILL NEVER AGAIN THINK OF SOMETHING AS IMPOSSIBLE . . .' THE SENATE CAMPAIGN OF 1972

1. The youngest age at which someone can take a seat in the Senate is 30. Biden was 29 at the time of the election, not celebrating his 30th birthday until a few weeks after it.

2. Nixon, Kennedy's old sparring partner, had finally won the White House in 1968 and was himself standing for re-election in 1972.

3. Biden's wife, Neilia, was heavily involved in planning and delivering the campaign, despite him having earlier told an interviewer that her role in the family should be to stay home to 'mold my children. I'm not a "keep 'em barefoot and pregnant" man but I am all for keeping them pregnant until I have a little girl . . . the only good thing in the world is kids.'

4. Biden's was, however, in favour of busing in places such as the Deep South, where segregation had been enforced by law, just not in his own state where he argued it was just a by-product of

people's decisions about where to live. See chapter 7 for more on Biden's position on desegregation busing.

5. In one of his most impassioned speeches, at the Democratic National Convention in June 1972, he implored his audience, 'for God's sake stop the Madison Avenue, sugar-coated garbage. Don't talk to us about a generation of peace when every day hundreds of planes cut through the skies of Indochina, and countless women and children and old men run from their liberators, their flesh burned with napalm.'

6. Now that Biden himself is one of the elder statesmen of US politics, he might not like to be reminded how much his advertising in 1972 traded on the generational gap between himself and his opponent. One advert read, 'Cale Boggs's generation dreamed of conquering polio. Joe Biden's generation dreams of conquering heroin . . . Joe Biden: he understands what's happening today.'

7. Nixon comprehensively defeated the Democratic challenger, George McGovern, winning in every single state bar Massachusetts.

5. 'WE WERE ON TOP OF THE WORLD AND THEN THE WORLD ENDED . . .' THE CRASH

1. The newly elected Governor of Delaware would have had responsibility for selecting another senator if Biden had quit.

6. 'DEATH AND THE ALL-AMERICAN BOY . . .' BIDEN'S EARLY YEARS IN THE SENATE

1. He went on to explain further, 'I don't like the Supreme Court decision on abortion. I think it went too far. I don't think that a woman has the sole right to say what should happen to her body. I support a limited amnesty, and I don't think marijuana should be legalized. Now, if you still think I'm a liberal, let me tell you that I support the draft. I'm scared to death of a professional army. I vote my own way and it is not always with the Democrats.'

2. Inflation and unemployment are normally considered opposing forces in economics, as high inflation is normally linked to high spending, which creates jobs.

7. 'A LIBERAL TRAIN WRECK . . .' THE DESEGREGATION BUSING CONTROVERSY

1. Jim Crow was a derogatory term for African Americans, derived from a popular 19th-century song mocking black people called 'Jump Jim Crow'.
2. Jacobs gave her reason for refusing Biden's repeated proposals as her not wanting to risk Hunter and Beau losing a second mother if the marriage didn't work out. She was eventually won over, according to one version of the story, by the boys themselves proposing to her.

8. 'TO MY GENERATION HAS NOW COME THE CHALLENGE . . .' JOE BIDEN'S 1980S

1. JFK's younger brother, Robert 'Bobby' Kennedy, had also been assassinated whilst running for president in 1968.

9. 'IN MY ZEAL TO REKINDLE IDEALISM, I HAVE MADE MISTAKES . . .' THE COLLAPSE OF BIDEN'S FIRST PRESIDENTIAL BID

1. Benjamin Hooks of the National Association for the Advancement of Colored People said of Bork's appointment, 'We will fight it . . . until hell freezes over, and then we'll skate across on the ice.'
2. Dukakis went on to lose the 1988 election to Reagan's Vice President, George H.W. Bush. Biden later met Kinnock in London in early 1988, the two men becoming friends. Many years later, Biden introduced Kinnock to his senate staff as "my greatest speechwriter" and invited him to attend Barack Obama's inauguration in 2008.

10. 'HAD HE STAYED IN THE RACE HE'D BE DEAD ALREADY . . .' FROM THE LAST RITES TO THE WORLD STAGE

1. Strom Thurmond, the most senior Republican on the Committee and a supporter of Thomas, did not pass the information about the allegations on to his party colleagues.
2. Clinton's election victory over Bush in 1992 brought an end to a period of near-total Republican domination of the White House. The Republicans had won every presidential election since 1968 with the sole exception of Carter's win in 1976.
3. Violent crime in the US dropped by 46% in the period from 1994 to 2017.
4. The act brought new attention to crimes that had been traditionally swept under the carpet in the US, including domestic violence, marital and date rape, and stalking.
5. At around the same time, Biden also pushed successfully for the expansion of NATO to include central and eastern European countries who had previously been on the other side of the 'iron curtain'.

11. 'I WOULD NOT BE ANYBODY'S VICE PRESIDENT, PERIOD . . .' FROM 9/11 TO BIDEN'S SECOND PRESIDENTIAL BID

1. Bush had won election in the year 2000 against Clinton's vice president, Al Gore, in the closest and most controversial election in modern American political history.
2. Even before 9/11, the newly elected President Bush had turned to Biden for advice prior to his first-ever visit to Europe.
3. Over the 19 years of conflict since 2001, the United States has discovered what the Soviets, and, before them, the British Empire, had already learned: that the mountainous and battle-hardened land of Afghanistan is nearly impossible to fully subjugate.
4. Biden made other comments about Obama that he must have come to regret in the run-up to the 2008 election, telling reporters, 'I think he can be ready [for the Presidency] but right now I don't believe he is. The presidency is not something that lends itself to on the job training.'

5. Biden put his foot in his mouth again on the same campaign trail when commenting on the growth of the Indian-American population in Delaware, saying, 'You cannot go to a 7-Eleven or a Dunkin' Donuts unless you have a slight Indian accent.'

12. 'CHANGE HAS COME TO AMERICA . . .' THE OBAMA-BIDEN 2008 CAMPAIGN

1. The Chief Strategist for Obama's campaigns, David Axelrod, said of Biden, 'Everyone's strength is also their weakness, and Joe Biden's strength is that he's real, he's genuine, he's ebullient . . . and he's credible as a result. The flip side of that is that he sometimes goes on some . . .'

2. Biden's most memorable moment in the debates came, atypically for him, with a single word. When the moderator put it to him that he had frequently talked himself into trouble with his unrestrained way with words and asked him, 'Can you reassure voters in this country that you would have the discipline you would need on the world stage, Senator?' Biden simply replied, 'Yes', and said no more, to the great amusement of his fellow candidates and the audience.

3. In the event of a President dying in office, resigning, or being forced out through impeachment, the vice president is automatically elevated to the top job.

4. The story about Biden's house being bought by an MBNA Executive had featured in a previous Republican campaign for Biden's senate seat. Accusations that the executive paid over the odds for Biden's house were subsequently shown to be untrue.

5. By the end of the 1990s, 4 of the 5 biggest credit card companies in the US were based in Wilmington, taking advantage of Delaware's notoriously corporate-friendly laws.

13. 'THE SKUNK AT THE FAMILY PICNIC . . .' BIDEN'S FIRST TERM AS VICE PRESIDENT

1. According to Leslie Gelb, the co-creator with Biden of the federation plan, "The Middle East experts in Washington all pissed on it."

2. $787 billion was the initial estimate for the cost of the package,

which has since been revised upwards to a total spend of $831 billion in the decade from 2009 to 2019.

3. Obama got 51% of the popular vote (compared to Romney's 47%) and took 332 electoral college votes to Romney's 206.

JOE BIDEN'S 2020 POLICIES

1. The definition is from the Education Commission of the States.